DATE DUE

JUL 3 1 2012		
OCT 0 4 2012		
NOV 15 2012		
JUL 16 2013		
SEP 25 2013		
SEP 1 6 2015		
SEP 2 0 2015		
DEC 1 2 2016		

Demco, Inc. 38-293

1st EDITION

Perspectives on Diseases and Disorders

Fibromyalgia

Sylvia Engdahl

Book Editor

GALE
CENGAGE Learning

Detroit • New York • San Francisco • New Haven, Conn • Waterville, Maine • London

Christine Nasso, *Publisher*
Elizabeth Des Chenes, *Managing Editor*

© 2010 Greenhaven Press, a part of Gale, Cengage Learning

For more information, contact:
Greenhaven Press
27500 Drake Rd.
Farmington Hills, MI 48331-3535
Or you can visit our Internet site at gale.cengage.com

For product information and technology assistance, contact us at

Gale Customer Support, 1-800-877-4253
For permission to use material from this text or product, submit all requests online at www.cengage.com/permissions

Further permissions questions can be emailed to permissionrequest@cengage.com

Articles in Greenhaven Press anthologies are often edited for length to meet page requirements. In addition, original titles of these works are changed to clearly present the main thesis and to explicitly indicate the author's opinion. Every effort is made to ensure that Greenhaven Press accurately reflects the original intent of the authors. Every effort has been made to trace the owners of copyrighted material.

Cover image © David Gee 2/Alamy

LIBRARY OF CONGRESS CATALOGING-IN-PUBLICATION DATA

Fibromyalgia / Sylvia Engdahl, book editor.
    p. cm. -- (Perspectives on diseases and disorders)
Includes bibliographical references and index.
ISBN 978-0-7377-5000-3 (hardcover)
1. Fibromyalgia. 2. Fibromyalgia--Treatment. I. Engdahl, Sylvia.
RC927.3F484 2010
616.7'42--dc22
                                                            2010010745

Printed in the United States of America
1 2 3 4 5 6 7 14 13 12 11 10

CONTENTS

treatments. Physicians who prescribe such drugs feel that these companies are limiting access to necessary medicine simply to decrease costs.

FOREWORD

"Medicine, to produce health, has to examine disease."
—Plutarch

Independent research on a health issue is often the first step to complement discussions with a physician. But locating accurate, well-organized, understandable medical information can be a challenge. A simple Internet search on terms such as "cancer" or "diabetes," for example, returns an intimidating number of results. Sifting through the results can be daunting, particularly when some of the information is inconsistent or even contradictory. The Greenhaven Press series Perspectives on Diseases and Disorders offers a solution to the often overwhelming nature of researching diseases and disorders.

From the clinical to the personal, titles in the Perspectives on Diseases and Disorders series provide students and other researchers with authoritative, accessible information in unique anthologies that include basic information about the disease or disorder, controversial aspects of diagnosis and treatment, and first-person accounts of those impacted by the disease. The result is a well-rounded combination of primary and secondary sources that, together, provide the reader with a better understanding of the disease or disorder.

Each volume in Perspectives on Diseases and Disorders explores a particular disease or disorder in detail. Material for each volume is carefully selected from a wide range of sources, including encyclopedias, journals, newspapers, nonfiction books, speeches, government documents, pamphlets, organization newsletters, and position papers. Articles in the first chapter provide an authoritative, up-to-date overview that covers symptoms, causes and effects, treatments, cures, and medical advances. The second chapter presents a substantial number of opposing viewpoints on controversial treatments and other current debates relating to the volume topic. The third chapter offers a variety of personal perspectives on the disease or disorder. Patients, doctors, caregivers, and loved ones represent just some of the voices found in this narrative chapter.

Each Perspectives on Diseases and Disorders volume also includes:

- An **annotated table of contents** that provides a brief summary of each article in the volume.
- An **introduction** specific to the volume topic.
- Full-color **charts and graphs** to illustrate key points, concepts, and theories.
- Full-color **photos** that show aspects of the disease or disorder and enhance textual material.
- **"Fast Facts"** that highlight pertinent additional statistics and surprising points.
- A **glossary** providing users with definitions of important terms.
- A **chronology** of important dates relating to the disease or disorder.
- An annotated list of **organizations to contact** for students and other readers seeking additional information.
- A **bibliography** of additional books and periodicals for further research.
- A detailed **subject index** that allows readers to quickly find the information they need.

Whether a student researching a disorder, a patient recently diagnosed with a disease, or an individual who simply wants to learn more about a particular disease or disorder, a reader who turns to Perspectives on Diseases and Disorders will find a wealth of information in each volume that offers not only basic information, but also vigorous debate from multiple perspectives.

INTRODUCTION

Fibromyalgia is a common medical condition about which little has been known until recently. It involves chronic muscular pain without inflammation or damage to the muscles, and in many cases includes other symptoms such as abnormal sensitivity to pain upon being touched, extreme fatigue, sleep disorders, and more. Because there are no biochemical tests that can detect fibromyalgia, it is difficult to diagnose and can be confirmed only by ruling out other disorders. Doctors disagree about the criteria for determining who has the condition, and sometimes people suffer for years before being told it is the cause of their pain.

Some, but not all, fibromyalgia patients have cognitive difficulties they call "fibro fog" in addition to their physical symptoms. However, fibromyalgia is not a psychiatric condition. In the past it was commonly said to be entirely psychological, and a few doctors still believe this, but the condition was never thought to be a sign of mental illness. Rather, the pain was assumed to be purely imaginary, and those who reported it were assumed to be hypochondriacs. When no physical abnormality in their bodies could be detected, they were told that it was "all in their heads." Those suffering from fibromyalgia became angry about this, since their bodies hurt just as much as if the trouble were not invisible. Today, the pain is generally acknowledged to be real, although what causes the condition is not yet understood and the theories that attempt to explain it are controversial.

Some of the controversy is based on confusion over terminology. Most doctors believe that fibromyalgia is at least partially the result of psychological factors, and the word "psychosomatic" is sometimes used. But "psychosomatic" does not mean "imaginary," as many people erroneously think. On the contrary, the term "psychosomatic"—which comes from the Greek words for "mind" and "body"—originally referred to *physical* changes in the body produced by psychological stress. That emotion does have physical effects is obvious: Everyone knows that being excited can lead to a rapidly beating heart and cold chills, for instance, and since this is common, it is considered normal. For some years scientists have been discovering other effects of the mind on the body that are less common, so effects of that kind possibly play a role in fibromyalgia. Specialists in mind/body research now usually avoid the word "psychosomatic" because it is so widely misunderstood. Whatever term is used, the effects they study are unquestionably real. Furthermore, psychological factors alone cannot explain why a person has the particular physical symptoms of fibromyalgia. Everybody experiences psychological stress, and the fact that different people's bodies react to it in different ways shows that physical factors must influence the effects that it has on them.

Another problem with terminology concerns the word "disease." There is a good deal of argument over the question of whether fibromyalgia is a "real disease," some of it sparked by a 2008 *New York Times* article that implied that it is not. However, not all conditions needing treatment are diseases. Most authorities call fibromyalgia a syndrome rather than a disease, which does not make it any less real. According to the explanation of fibromyalgia from the National Institutes of Health, "A syndrome is a collection of signs, symptoms, and medical problems that tend to occur together but are not related to a specific, identifiable cause. A disease, on the other hand, has a specific cause or causes and recognizable signs and symptoms." Many discussions of fibromyalgia refer to it as FMS, or fibromyalgia syndrome.

Currently, more and more researchers are coming to believe that the pain of fibromyalgia is due to a neurological problem. Evidence suggests that the brains of FMS patients do not process pain in the same way as those of other people. This theory does not account for all the other symptoms associated with the syndrome or the fact that some patients have only muscular pain without general hypersensitivity to pain, but it is a step toward understanding the condition.

No statistics about the prevalence of FMS are available because the diagnostic criteria vary and because many sufferers do not seek medical attention. Estimates suggest that it affects 3 million to 6 million people in the United States. The vast majority of those diagnosed with it are women. However, men do get it, and some researchers believe a larger percentage of men are affected than records show because they are less likely than women to see a doctor about the condition. Some teens, and even children, also have fibromyalgia, though for it to develop in youth is relatively uncommon.

Although fibromyalgia cannot be cured, now certain treatments are helping some patients. Several drugs have been approved for it during the past few years, but they do not work for everyone, and they have undesirable side effects. Treating sleep disorders is often helpful. And a wide variety of "alternative medicine" treatments such as acupuncture or yoga are beneficial to some.

Nevertheless, many people's lives are profoundly affected by FMS. The severity of its symptoms varies widely from individual to individual. In some patients they occur only periodically; in others they are constant. It is never fatal, but like other forms of chronic pain it can cause disability, sometimes permanent disability, even though it does no actual damage to the body.

Recently, many fibromyalgia patients have become activists and are promoting public awareness of FMS. They

Women make up the vast majority of fibromyalgia sufferers. The disorder has no known cure. (© Jonathan Miller/Alamy)

are encouraged by increased medical recognition of the syndrome, but they often find that people with whom they associate do not realize that they are truly ill. As their condition is invisible to observers whether or not it has been officially diagnosed, they have trouble getting insurance to cover treatment and getting disability payments if they are unable to work. Sometimes not even their families understand their limitations. And they feel that the low visibility of the disorder has resulted in too little effort and funding being devoted to the search for a cure.

Hundreds of Web sites are devoted to fibromyalgia. Some are maintained by support or research organizations, others by large pharmaceutical companies, and still others by people with the condition who want to help fellow sufferers. Also, many sites that appear to contain authoritative information are actually selling or promoting products or treatments that are not based on scientific research and are not widely accepted. Some such treatments do help some individuals, but claims that they will help most patients, or that the cause of fibromyalgia has been discovered, are not valid. If a treatment could eliminate FMS symptoms in the majority of cases, doctors and legitimate support organizations would soon know about it.

The information about fibromyalgia found online should be carefully evaluated and the sources' legitimacy should be assessed. Hopefully, effective treatments for all the symptoms of FMS will eventually be developed. But at present, it is a chronic condition with which patients must learn to live.

CHAPTER 1

Understanding Fibromyalgia

An Overview of Fibromyalgia

Dale Guyer, interviewed by Joan SerVaas

In the following article Joan SerVaas interviews Dale Guyer, who treats many fibromyalgia patients. Guyer relates that many Americans suffer from the disease and the cause remains unknown. He describes the symptoms of the disease and how the disorder is diagnosed. SerVaas is the chief executive officer and publisher of the *Saturday Evening Post*, a bimonthly American magazine.

M uscle pain is only part of the problem facing millions of Americans living with fibromyalgia, a condition virtually unheard of 20 years ago. A thorough medical evaluation can often point to helpful strategies for dealing with the chronic ailment.

Day in and day out, millions of Americans wake up to debilitating musculoskeletal pain and severe fatigue. Until recently, physicians were perplexed by the mysterious

Photo on previous page. Fibromyalgia causes pain in the muscles, tendons, ligaments, and other soft, fibrous tissues of the body and has been linked to a disorder of the nervous system. (Jim Dowdalls/Photo Researchers, Inc)

SOURCE: Joan SerVaas, "Focus on Fibromyalgia," *Saturday Evening Post*, March/April 2000, p. 56. Copyright © 2000 Saturday Evening Post Society. Reproduced by permission.

illness because objective, physiologic evidence from x-rays, blood tests, and other diagnostic screenings looked normal. The patient's symptoms were frequently attributed to psychological origins.

During the past decade, however, researchers have discovered that the symptoms are linked to a very real ailment known as fibromyalgia, estimated to affect some 3 million Americans, most of whom are women between 20 and 50 years old. Fibromyalgia refers to pain in the muscles, ligaments, and tendons in the body. Although muscular pain and fatigue are hallmarks of the disorder, other symptoms include irritable bowel syndrome, chronic headaches, temporomandibular joint dysfunction, and chemical sensitivity syndrome, among others. . . .

The *Post* interviewed Dr. Dale Guyer, who treats many patients with fibromyalgia and chronic fatigue syndrome in his clinic.

Joan SerVaas [Post]. Fibromyalgia is getting much more attention from doctors who treat the disorder and the individuals who suffer from it. What is fibromyalgia? Is it related to chronic fatigue syndrome?

Dale Guyer. We often find in many people that chronic fatigue syndrome and fibromyalgia are intertwined. Some people express more in one direction than the other. In my practice, many people have elements of both disorders.

Fibromyalgia is frequently described as a general "hurting all over." There are specific diagnostic criteria involving 11 out of 18 tender points on different areas of the body, starting at the base of the skull and involving the back, the inner arms, thighs, and so forth. In addition, fibromyalgia usually lasts longer than three months and is often accompanied by sleep disturbances and other miscellaneous symptoms. People with fibromyalgia may also complain of fatigue that at times warrants a diagnosis of chronic fatigue syndrome.

Chronic fatigue is a generalized, debilitating, long-standing fatigue that dramatically encroaches into a person's ability to participate in the activities of daily living.

SerVaas. What are tender points?

Guyer. Tender points in fibromyalgia are part of the diagnostic criteria. Many people don't even recognize that they have tender points until a doctor actually pushes on those points. Patients can literally jump off the table because these areas are so tender....

SerVaas. What causes fibromyalgia and chronic fatigue syndrome?

Guyer. We really don't know as yet the cause of chronic fatigue or fibromyalgia. Typically, we first exclude other potential diagnoses, such as autoimmune disorders, digestive disorders, musculoskeletal problems, and even

An illustration shows fibromyalgia symptoms and trigger points on the human body.
(© **Nucleus Medical Art, Inc.**/Alamy)

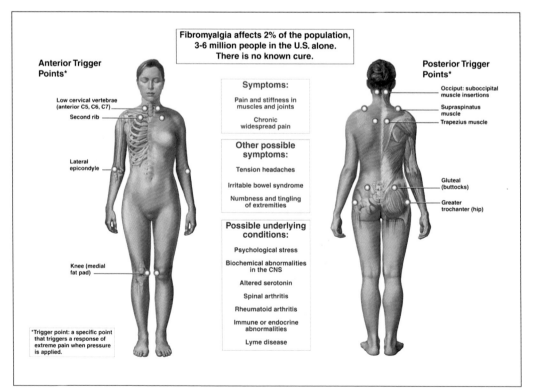

Fibromyalgia affects 2% of the population, 3-6 million people in the U.S. alone. There is no known cure.

Anterior Trigger Points*

Low cervical vertebrae (anterior C5, C6, C7)

Second rib

Lateral epicondyle

Knee (medial fat pad)

*Trigger point: a specific point that triggers a response of extreme pain when pressure is applied.

Symptoms:

Pain and stiffness in muscles and joints

Chronic widespread pain

Other possible symptoms:

Tension headaches

Irritable bowel syndrome

Numbness and tingling of extremities

Possible underlying conditions:

Psychological stress

Biochemical abnormalities in the CNS

Altered serotonin

Spinal arthritis

Rheumatoid arthritis

Immune or endocrine abnormalities

Lyme disease

Posterior Trigger Points*

Occiput: suboccipital muscle insertions

Supraspinatus muscle

Trapezius muscle

Gluteal (buttocks)

Greater trochanter (hip)

cancers can sometimes mimic some symptoms of chronic fatigue and fibromyalgia. After we exclude other disorders, we can more comfortably diagnose fibromyalgia or chronic fatigue syndrome as a diagnosis of exclusion.

Therapy for both generally focuses on symptom control. Anti-inflammatories may help with pain; stimulants sometimes help improve energy, and other medicines improve sleep. Certain antidepressant drugs, such as Prozac and Serzone, often help with the depression that many people with these conditions feel, and the antidepressants can improve some patients' pain control.

SerVaas. What are some of the most common complaints and characteristics of this syndrome in cases that you see?

Guyer. With my patients, I do a global evaluation to understand underlying problems. For example, if we were looking at someone with chronic fatigue syndrome and fibromyalgia, we would look at what is going on metabolically with the individual. I often see low thyroid function, endocrine abnormalities, hormonal problems, deficiencies (even for women) of testosterone and DHEA [hormone similar to testosterone], adrenal insufficiency, accumulation of toxic metals. Many individuals will measure quite high on toxic metals that may play a very strong inflammatory role, such as aluminum, cadmium, mercury, and lead.

Low thyroid function is commonly associated with chronic fatigue and fibromyalgia, even though results from lab tests are within normal range; the levels are often low normal. Lab tests only measure a hormone level; they don't really tell you anything about the functional state or activity of the hormone. The tests don't tell you even how receptive your body's tissues are to the thyroid hormones.

> **FAST FACT**
>
> According to statistics released by the American College of Rheumatology, fibromyalgia (FM) affects 3 million to 6 million people in the United States, but other estimates vary. As of 2009, the National Fibromyalgia Association estimated that 10 million Americans had FM.

Prominent Symptoms Associated with Fibromyalgia

In a study of 293 patients, 158 were diagnosed with fibromyalgia; 135, the control patients, did not meet the criteria as described by the America College of Rheumatology.

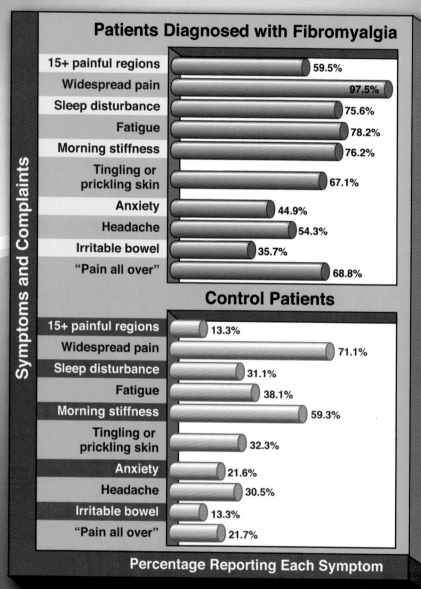

Patients Diagnosed with Fibromyalgia

Symptoms and Complaints

Symptom	Percentage
15+ painful regions	59.5%
Widespread pain	97.5%
Sleep disturbance	75.6%
Fatigue	78.2%
Morning stiffness	76.2%
Tingling or prickling skin	67.1%
Anxiety	44.9%
Headache	54.3%
Irritable bowel	35.7%
"Pain all over"	68.8%

Control Patients

Symptom	Percentage
15+ painful regions	13.3%
Widespread pain	71.1%
Sleep disturbance	31.1%
Fatigue	38.1%
Morning stiffness	59.3%
Tingling or prickling skin	32.3%
Anxiety	21.6%
Headache	30.5%
Irritable bowel	13.3%
"Pain all over"	21.7%

Percentage Reporting Each Symptom

Taken from: Frederick Wolfe, et al., "The American College of Rheumatology 1990 Criteria for the Classification of Fibromyalgia: Report of the Multicenter Criteria Committee," *Arthritis and Rheumatism*, vol. 33, no. 2, February 1990, p. 165.

When we determine what a normal laboratory value is for a particular test, in this case thyroid hormone levels, we are sampling the general population. From that mass sampling, we determine what is average. But if we are sampling many people out there, many of them don't feel well. A list of thyroid symptoms includes: fatigue, PMS, dry skin, brittle nails, weight gain, difficulty with weight loss, depression, low motivation, feeling cold all the time, and constipation. In my practice I've seen a number of individuals with thyroid symptoms, and yet their lab tests were normal. A low dose of a natural thyroid extract, such as Armour Thyroid, can literally be life-changing in many of these patients.

Infectious processes can also be involved. Certain types of fungi—such as *Candida albicans*, other bacterial organisms, imbalances in the digestive tract of friendly and unfriendly bacteria, poor digestive process, immune dysfunction problems—may be involved. We can often measure viral problems, such as Epstein-Barr virus, HHV6 (human herpesvirus type 6), CMV [cytomegalovirus], and others that have a clear association. Evaluating the nutritional status is also important. Many people with fibromyalgia display a nutritional deficit in minerals, such as magnesium or calcium, as well as deficiencies in some of their antioxidants—especially coenzyme [Q_{10}] and vitamin E.

During the evaluation, you begin to understand what areas are imbalanced in an individual. You can then correct the imbalance by giving the body what it is lacking. In this way, you create a body environment conducive to health and healing. The body is usually quite capable of taking care of itself. Our goal is only to provide the environment for that natural reaction to occur.

Physicians with Different Specialties Treat Fibromyalgia Differently

Sherry Boschert

In the following article Sherry Boschert discusses a survey that shows that different doctors use different diagnostic tests for fibromyalgia and prescribe different treatments. A large fraction of them do not follow the American College of Rheumatology (ACR) diagnostic criteria, she claims, although more rheumatologists than primary care physicians do so. Moreover, the doctor who presented the data at an ACR meeting believes that it is important to determine which tests are best because they are expensive and because there should be standards for diagnosis. Boschert is a senior reporter and San Francisco bureau chief of the International Medical News Group.

Rheumatologists and primary care physicians tend to use different diagnostic tests and prescribe different treatments for fibromyalgia syndrome, survey results indicated.

SOURCE: Sherry Boschert, "Fibromyalgia Care Varies Among Specialties," *Internal Medicine News*, vol. 42, January 1, 2009, p. 22. Copyright © 2009 International Medical News Group. Reproduced by permission.

A large fraction of physicians in both groups did not follow the American College of Rheumatology (ACR) 1990 criteria for diagnosing fibromyalgia, Dr. Terence W. Starz and his associates reported in a poster presentation at the annual meeting of the American College of Rheumatology.

"I don't know what that means," conceded Dr. Starz, a rheumatologist at the University of Pittsburgh Medical Center. "We've got to adhere to criteria" to develop standards of care, he said in an interview during the poster session.

Questionnaires e-mailed to 199 rheumatologists throughout Pennsylvania and 183 primary care physicians in the southwestern portion of the state were returned by 74 (37%) of the rheumatologists and 89 (49%) of the primary care physicians. Both groups agreed that it takes more time to manage patients with fibromyalgia than other patients.

A primary care physician checks a patient for fibromyalgia trigger points. Rheumatologists and primary care physicians often diagnose the disorder differently. (Robin Conn/The Huntsville Times/Landov)

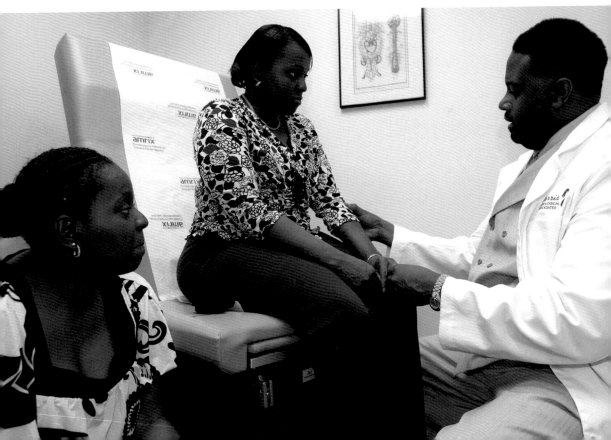

Rheumatologists were significantly more likely to use ACR criteria to diagnose fibromyalgia (56, or 76%) compared with primary care physicians (50, or 56%). The two groups also differed significantly in the use of tests to measure levels of vitamin D, rheumatoid factor, antinuclear antibody, and anti-cyclic citrullinated peptide (anti-CCP) antibody. They reported similar rates of testing for thyroid function, metabolic profile, and human leukocyte antigen B27.

FAST FACT

Fibromyalgia occurs worldwide in all ethnic groups and cultures. In 1993 the World Health Organization officially recognized it as a diagnosis.

"We need to determine which ones of those should be utilized, because they're very expensive. A vitamin D level can cost up to $250. Anti-CCP is very expensive. They're not included" in the current ACR diagnostic criteria, Dr. Starz said. "We, as a discipline, need to set out standards for diagnosis."

Vitamin D levels were ordered by 36 rheumatologists (49%) and 15 primary care physicians (17%). Tests for rheumatoid factor were ordered by 43 (58%) and 68 (76%), respectively. Rheumatologists were more likely to measure anti-CCP level (24, or 32%) than were primary care physicians (5, or 6%) but less likely to test for antinuclear antibody (45, or 61%, compared with 68, or 76%, of primary care physicians).

Doctors' Perceptions of Fibromyalgia

The two groups reported similar perceptions about the pathophysiology of fibromyalgia. Approximately three-fourths said fibromyalgia is both a medical and psychological condition, less than 20% said it's solely a medical condition, and less than 10% said it's solely a psychological condition, judging from the findings in the research, which was recognized as a "notable poster" by the ACR.

Nearly all physicians in both groups prescribed exercise and physical therapy to treat fibromyalgia, but their use of most other therapies differed significantly.

Tender Points in Fibromyalgia

Diagnostic criteria developed in 1990 by the American College of Rheumatology characterize fibromyalgia syndrome as widespread pain in all regions of the body and pain to the touch in at least eleven of the eighteen spots identified in the illustration.

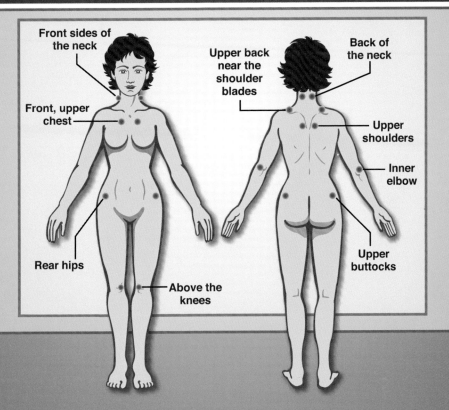

Front sides of the neck

Upper back near the shoulder blades

Back of the neck

Front, upper chest

Upper shoulders

Inner elbow

Rear hips

Upper buttocks

Above the knees

Taken from: Fibromyalgia and Fatigue Centers, Incorporated, "Fibromyalgia Tender Points." www.fibromyalgia.tenderpoints.org.

Cognitive therapy was prescribed by 39 rheumatologists (52%) and 26 primary care physicians (29%). NSAIDs [nonsteroidal anti-inflammatory drugs] were prescribed by 42 (57%) of the rheumatologists and favored by primary care physicians (75, or 84%). "The data on NSAIDs, though, are not very good for fibromyalgia," Dr. Starz said.

The primary care physicians also were significantly more likely to use SSRIs [selective serotonin reuptake inhibitors] (68, or 76%) compared with rheumatologists (42, or 57%).

Rheumatologists were more likely to treat with cyclobenzaprine [an antidepressant] (64, or 86%), or alpha-2-delta ligands [anticonvulsants] such as gabapentin or pregabalin (64, of 86%), compared with primary care physicians (50, or 56% and 59, or 66%, respectively).

The use of selective norepinephrine reuptake inhibitors for fibromyalgia was similar between groups.

"What's interesting to me is there's not nearly enough focus on sleep hygiene and sleep treatment" for patients with fibromyalgia, Dr. Starz commented.

An estimated 5 million people in the United States have fibromyalgia syndrome, more than the combined total of patients with rheumatoid arthritis (1.3 million), systemic lupus erythematosus (322,000), scleroderma (49,000), polymyalgia rheumatica (228,000), and gout (3 million), he said.

Fibromyalgia Has Not Yet Been Clearly Defined

M. Clement Hall

In the following excerpt from his book *The Fibromyalgia Controversy*, M. Clement Hall lists what is known about the pain of fibromyalgia and concludes that the American College of Rheumatology (ACR) diagnostic criteria, which were originally developed only for use in research and were disputed even at the time, are not a reliable means of defining the disorder. Hall asserts that these criteria identify only a portion of the patients who have chronic widespread pain. He explains that although some people believe a condition with no physical signs must be merely a mental one, the mind is now known to bring about chemical changes in the central nervous system, so that even if pain has an emotional origin, it is real. All patients with chronic widespread pain should be given the diagnosis of fibromyalgia, he says, and treatment should be based on distress with the aim of keeping the patient functioning. Hall, now retired, was the director of continuing education in the Emergency Department of Scarborough Hospital in Toronto, Canada.

SOURCE: M. Clement Hall, *The Fibromyalgia Controversy*. Amherst, NY: Prometheus Books, 2009. Copyright © 2009 by M. Clement Hall. All rights reserved. Reproduced by permission.

This is what has been established so far:

- There are five million persons in the United States bearing the diagnosis of fibromyalgia.
- They are nearly all women, although there is a juvenile form.
- The criteria for diagnosis were promulgated in 1990. They were disputed at the time and remain in dispute.
- The purpose in defining criteria was to set an agreed base point for research into the issue of patients with

Levels Along a Spectrum of Chronic Muscular Pain

Regional distinctions for muscular and connective tissue pain can be identified as the upper left, upper right, lower left, and lower right sides of the body. A diagnosis of widespread pain disorder necessitates pain in all four regions of the body, but a true fibromyalgia patient must also suffer from pain of the spine, pain to the touch at specific points, fatigue, and sleep disturbances.

Chronic regional pain syndrome (e.g., chronic back pain)

Multiregional pain syndrome (e.g., chronic neck, back, and shoulder pain)

Widespread pain syndrome

Fibromyalgia syndrome

Increasing pain, stiffness, fatigue, and sleep disturbances

Taken from: Greg Fors, *Why We Hurt: A Complete Physical and Spiritual Guide to Healing Your Chronic Pain*. Woodbury, MN: Llewellyn, 2007, p. 316.

widespread pain and to set criteria to separate "real" clinical cases from "unreal" neurasthenics.

- Not intended by the members of the 1990 committee, these criteria have become fixed and unwavering determinants for who does and who does not qualify for a "real" diagnosis, named fibromyalgia.
- The diagnosis of fibromyalgia has become representative of a permanent and disabling condition and a foundation for disability awards, including civil litigation.
- The only required feature of the history is the patient's unverifiable report of chronic widespread pain.
- The only required feature of the physical examination is the patient's unverifiable complaint of pain when four kg [kilograms] pressure is applied by the thumb at eleven of eighteen designated points. Ten of these designated points are above the nipple line.
- The position of these "tender points" is displayed in pictures of spotty ladies, widely available on the Internet and in popular books and magazines.
- The choice of the points was arbitrary, both in location and in numbers. These points are tender to everyone, but were expected from experience to be more tender than usual, in fact painful, to someone with fibromyalgia.
- The test was for an abnormal sensitivity to pain, or lowered pain threshold. There is no known abnormality in the tissues that are compressed, nor was it ever supposed that there was a tissue abnormality.
- Chronic widespread pain is now known to occur in the absence of tender points. No diagnostic term was applied to this state, which has remained up in the air as a complaint and not designated as a disease.
- Tender points are now known to occur in the absence of chronic widespread pain. No diagnostic term was applied to this state, which has also remained up in

the air as a complaint and not designated as a disease.

- In practical "real-life" terms, it is reported that many physicians, perhaps most outside university clinics, make their diagnosis on the basis of the history and either do not perform the tender point examination or may discount the results.

- It is suggested by the lead author of the 1990 report that the tender point examination is irrelevant to the diagnosis.

- Others, including that author, equate the tender point examination with the degree of the patient's distress.

- To some, the diagnostic approach has come full circle. The intention was to separate "real" from "unreal" and although most gave weight to the history, a physical test was devised as a *sine qua non* [essential].

- It is now known that this physical test is unreliable, in that there are false positives and false negatives, and it excludes from an important diagnosis a significant element of patients. In fact, this was known at the time, or shortly after, the test was established.

Three issues need to be addressed:

1. Persons diagnosed with fibromyalgia resent intensely and even abusively the removal of the physical construct of the diagnosis, with the thought that fibromyalgia is consequently designated as "other than physical," which is to say "it's all in your head."

2. Is fibromyalgia a unique disease, in and of itself?

3. If it is agreed the tender point examination, worthy intention though it might have been in 1990, is not a valid indicator of a separate condition, what Pandora's box does that open? It is estimated that if history alone were the basis, the number of persons qualifying for the diagnosis would be raised by two- or three-fold.

Patients Resent the Denial of a Physical Condition

If there is no physical sign, if there are symptoms but no signs, then to some persons the condition cannot be a physical one. It can be no more than emotional, which to some persons is tantamount to calling them a mental case. This conclusion ignores the invisibility of the pain associated with numerous conditions such as postherpetic neuralgia, tic douloureux, causalgia, diabetic neuropathy, and many others that have the advantage of social acceptability.

It is widely accepted that chemical and possibly physical changes occur in the central nervous system, neuroplasticity, resulting in an altered state of function called

Fibromyalgia sufferers are often told that their symptoms are imaginary, which leads to feelings of frustration and humiliation. (© PhotoAlto/Alamy)

neuropathy. These changes are signaled by sophisticated tests that show the presence of neurotransmitter chemicals to be found in patients suffering from fibromyalgia in quantifies that differ from those found in unaffected persons. Other sophisticated tests show altered functioning activity in the brains of persons with fibromyalgia, demonstrating their difference from healthy normal controls. There is no reason to suppose these changes cannot be reversed.

One can understand the urgency with which the patients insist their problem is physical and not emotional, but the weight attached by some researchers in the field when their conclusions are challenged, when they come to a forceful defense of their patients' viewpoint, is more suggestive of self-interested polemic than science.

These same researchers would serve their patients well if they were to go on the warpath on the bizarre modern concept of separation of mind and body. The ancient Chinese, Indians, and Greeks knew better, even today the witch doctor in central Africa knows better, but many Western physicians continue with this misapprehension. These biochemical tests of neurotransmitters measurably demonstrate the physical connection between mind and body. With PET [positron emission tomography] scans and fMRI [functional magnetic resonance imaging] the lucky few can actually watch the mind in action. There is no longer any defense for arguing whether a symptom is "only in the mind."

Is Fibromyalgia Really Unique?

There's a kind of a selfish streak to fibromyalgia. It seems almost as if sufferers are saying, "This is our disease—others keep out." Even the books written for the consumer talk "family" as do the networks and the blogs. Much of the research seems to be directed at proving a point, not at exploring a field to find what's there, but in proving a hypothesis that fibromyalgia is in some sense unique, leaving the work open to the criticism that the results are intended to please the customers—the customers of course being the researcher's own patients and the network supporting him. *(Noticeably a "him." Is this paternalistic?)*

The "tender points" was a well-meant idea, but a *faux pas*, a false step, conceptually fallacious, finding tender points in normal tissues and basing a diagnosis on finding pain where by definition there was no cause for pain. It's led the researchers into an impasse. . . . Some are unwilling to turn around and leave this blind alley. Others are reviled for doing so. But it makes no sense, and clinging to the well-intended mistake will not bring respect and will inevitably retard progress.

So what does that leave? It leaves all the symptoms of fibromyalgia, the distress, and the association with multiple other conditions. . . .

But is chronic widespread pain and distress unique? Is it peculiar to fibromyalgia? We know it's not.

The researchers have shown changes in neurochemistry and brain function in a small number of patients with fibromyalgia. People are funny. They're a bit reluctant to have needles stuck into their spines, so the ability to study cerebrospinal fluid and its circulating neurochemical transmitters is limited. MRI machines are expensive and usually they're expected to be revenue-earning; not many people have the luxury of using them for time-consuming research. So progress in learning is slow. And when opportunities are restricted, they'll be limited to a target group. We'll not know whether the observed neurochemical and brain-function changes are unique to fibromyalgia until it is shown they are not to be found in other cases of chronic widespread pain, nor in reflex sympathetic dystrophy, nor the multiple other forms of regional pain.

> **FAST FACT**
>
> Many researchers believe that fibromyalgia is the result of abnormalities in the way the brain and spinal cord process and transmit pain.

We do know changes of this nature are produced by both placebo and nocebo effects—further physical evidence of the mind-body inseparability. We have also learned over time that the alpha/delta sleep wave anomaly encountered in patients with fibromyalgia is in fact neither unique to that condition nor diagnostic of it.

So, no, nothing unique has been shown about fibromyalgia, except perhaps the expressed severity of the pain. . . .

The Broad Power of the Tender Point Examination

The original premise . . . was to separate the worst affected patients from others who could or would be classified as neurasthenics and seemingly less worthy of a diagnosis. This skimmed the top off the iceberg, granting the status of "real disease" to a minority (who jealously guard that privilege) and leaving the majority out in the cold without so much as a name to put to their symptoms, beyond, one supposes, "all in your head." Essentially this was the grossest form of discrimination, taking the loudest or most visible complainers, giving them status, and declining status to the balance. . . .

Pain and distress go hand in hand. There is no place for an Orwellian [referring to a saying in George Orwell's *Animal Farm*, "Some animals are more equal than others,"] "Some pains are more equal than others." The severity of the condition known as fibromyalgia has justified it being named. Other conditions of lesser severity of expressed pain and distress should not be excluded from that name.

Fully established fibromyalgia is the tip of the iceberg. The patient whose life revolves around her symptoms, who seeks on a regular basis the numerous non-traditional therapies, who has her own Internet blog describing in detail her daily travails and obscenely abuses the doctors who don't give her everything she demands, who after many rejections has now obtained permanent disability status supported by a pension—she is not going to be rehabilitated into functioning society. . . .

One doctor, after listening to her and examining her, will reassure her the pain is recent, not severe, probably of no consequence, and she should return if it persists. Another doctor will do the same in terms of history and examination but will order "tests." The tests are negative, which inevitably engenders more tests. The patient talks to her friends who make suggestions about CAT [computerized axial tomography] scans or MRIs or endoscopies. The doctor is obliged to conform to the suggestions. The doctor loses nothing by ordering them. She has an angry patient, and possibly her attorney to contend with, if she won't order them. . . . And down the slippery slope goes the cart. Into the slough of despond, and on from there to the door of the rheumatologist's office.

Fibromyalgia Must Be Prevented

Once established, experience has shown that fibromyalgia is difficult to eliminate or to minimize. The patient is not born with fibromyalgia. She doesn't catch it like chickenpox. It doesn't come suddenly. There's a tipping point at which her sensitive nature could either be sensitized and made fibromyalgic, or could be handled gently and kept in balance. Physicians learn about diseases, yet half or more of the persons they see in their offices have sensations that only become symptoms when the physician treats them as such. Every sensation reported must be assessed cautiously, but caution does not require exhaustive testing. It is not usual for the student to be taught most of the persons she sees with sensations will not be in need of physical treatment, and their sensations will surely turn into more-severe and deep-rooted symptoms if they are subjected to serial tests with predictable negative results, serial investigations by x-ray, MRI and ultrasound, and serial consultations. If they're fortunate these will all be reported as "nothing untoward found," but the statistical likelihood is some variation of normal will be exposed, resulting in more tests or even surgery. The tipping point is whether the physician embarks on this in the first place. That will depend on the physician's training, her confidence in her decision, and her support against medicolegal bullying.

The patient has a role to play. If the patient does not have confidence in her doctor or if she is determined to have that test she read about on the Internet or in the magazine, or her friends insist she has a "right" to receive, almost certainly she'll have it. It will be inconclusive. Then there'll be more. Then she'll seek out her own therapists and set up in control of her own treatment program. She'll find the "right" doctors who prescribe according to the Internet, she may even have found them from the Internet. She won't be happy. Her symptoms will magnify and multiply the more she reads and the more different forms of treatment she experiences, but she'll persuade herself she's "taken charge" of her pain. It won't be easy to stop this, but fibromyalgia will be alive and well as long as there are Internet sites, magazines, and therapists whose *raison d' être* [reason for being] lies in promotion and not prevention. . . .

The ACR criteria have "married" the profession to fibromyalgia. The diagnosis is recognized by WHO [World Health Organization], AMA [American Medical Association], ACR [American College of Rheumatology], EULAR [European League Against Rheumatism] and all the other alphabet soups. What is done is done. Now we have to find an exit strategy to deal with the *law of unforeseen consequences.*

It is incontestable that the "tender points" have become a nonsense as a diagnostic test, separating the *haves* from the *have-nots.* Separating fibromyalgia from other forms of chronic widespread pain. It is too late to abolish the diagnostic term "fibromyalgia," so I suggest retention of the term and extension of its application to all those distressed by pain who would qualify for the diagnosis except for failing the five-fifths distribution of pain or not matching up with the spotty ladies. In fact, these are probably the honest ones who haven't arranged their symptoms to match the well-known diagnostic requirements.

The suggestions are:
- Diagnose as "fibromyalgia" all those distressed with chronic widespread pain.
- Pick up the hidden part of the iceberg.
- Arrange appropriate treatment based on distress.
- Give up the sporadic symptom chasing treatment that is the norm today.
- Rethink primary contact medicine so such persons receive early appropriate care.
- In this way they will be prevented from reaching that irredeemable tip of the iceberg.
- Such care will be based on an understanding of neuropathic pain.
- Its prime direction will be to keep the patient functioning in her community.

Sleep Disorders May Play a Role in the Pain of Fibromyalgia

Regina Patrick

The following article from *Sleep Review* summarizes the debate about the causes of fibromyalgia and discusses the relationship between fibromyalgia and sleep. Regina Patrick reports that sleep disorders are common among people with fibromyalgia, and it is commonly thought that pain causes their insomnia. However, says the author, some studies indicate that fibromyalgia may be a manifestation of an intrinsic sleep disorder that results in both poor sleep and pain. People experimentally deprived of deep sleep develop symptoms similar to those of fibromyalgia. Not all scientists agree with this theory, Patrick reports; however, treating sleep disorders may help improve fibromyalgia symptoms. Patrick is a contributing writer for *Sleep Review* magazine.

Fibromyalgia (FM) is a chronic pain syndrome involving fatigue, morning stiffness, widespread muscle pain, cognitive problems, and poor sleep quality.

SOURCE: Regina Patrick, "The Fibromyalgia Debate," *Sleep Review*, November 2008, pp. 30, 32–3. Copyright © Allied Media LLC. Reproduced by permission.

It affects 2% to 4% of Americans. There appears to be no pathology such as inflammation or degenerative changes that could explain the symptoms of FM. This lack of pathology for many physicians suggests that an FM sufferer's pain may be psychological in origin (psychogenic). Other physicians believe that FM has a yet-to-be-determined physiological origin. Because neither side can definitively prove their stance, a continuing controversy exists . . . over whether FM is a "real" (ie, physiological) disease. In the midst of this irresolution, the US Food and Drug Administration (FDA) in June 2007 approved the drug pregabalin (trade name, Lyrica) to relieve pain in people with FM. Although other pain medications are prescribed for FM patients, pregabalin is the first that is specifically targeted for the unique pain of FM. While the development of a specific drug for FM pain is a tacit acknowledgment for physicians and FM patients who believe the disorder is physiological, other physicians in the medical community express concerns that a drug has been invented for a non-existent disease.

The Debate over FM's Legitimacy

Physicians who believe that FM is psychogenic have proposed several psychosocial factors to explain the pain. Some of the more common factors that have been proposed are: (1) a physician may be inadvertently inducing a patient's pain by validating it (in other words, FM may be an iatrogenic [treatment-induced] disorder); (2) social rewards such as disability compensation may promote an FM patient's being sick; (3) people with FM may be unusually susceptible to social pressures that groom them to be "sick"; and (4) people with FM may have weak coping skills for handling the normal stresses of everyday living.

Physicians who believe that fibromyalgia has a yet-to-be-determined physical origin counter that there are unique physiological characteristics noted in people with

Research has shown that fibromyalgia is often accompanied by sleep disorders. (Oscar Burriel/Photo Researchers, Inc.)

FM that are not noted in people without the disorder. For example, people with fibromyalgia have alpha-delta sleep (intrusion of alpha waves into delta sleep [also called slow wave sleep]); higher-than-normal levels of substance P, an algesic (pain-promoting) peptide that is thought to act as a neurotransmitter mediating touch, temperature, and sensation of pain; low cerebral spinal fluid level of the neurotransmitter 5-hydroxytryptophan and low blood level of the neurotransmitter tryptophan, which both play a role in pain perception and depression; and decreased blood flow in the thalami, which play a role in pain perception, and decreased cortical blood flow, which may explain fatigue and cognitive problems (eg, difficulty thinking, memory problems) noted by people with FM.

The Debate Leaves People with FM Hurting

As the medical community continues to debate the "realness" of FM, people with the disorder are left hurting not only physically but also in the following ways:

1) Because each side focuses on convincing the other that its perception concerning the "realness" of FM is correct, more energy is focused on persuasive arguments than is spent on proving or disproving hypotheses. As a result, new avenues of treatment are potentially not investigated.

2) FM patients feel discounted when a physician treats the pain as "only psychological." The sense of being discounted adds to the emotional distress already occurring with the chronic pain.

3) Some physicians, believing that the disorder is more psychogenic than physiological, refuse to treat people with FM or may do a one-time assessment to rule out other disorders but will not provide ongoing care. With physicians refusing to treat FM patients, this potentially means many FM sufferers have been prevented from receiving effective ongoing care.

In 1990, FM seemed to be on the way to being accepted as a "real" disease when the American College of Rheumatology (ACR) Multicenter Criteria Committee, headed by Dr Frederick Wolfe, established the diagnostic criteria now used for fibromyalgia. The diagnostic features consist of only two criteria [1.) long-term persistent pain in specified spots and 2.) tenderness at 11 or 18 designated points, at the least] that had to exist before a person is diagnosed with FM.

Second-Guessing Diagnostic Criteria

By 2003, Wolfe had begun expressing second thoughts about these criteria, especially the tender point criterion. One problem is that this criterion describes FM in terms of its severity rather than describing the features of the illness. To require that a person had to have at least 11 tender points is like—to use Wolfe's analogy—requiring a person with rheumatoid arthritis to have 25 swollen joints before diagnosing rheumatoid arthritis. He further points out that many people with FM may be overlooked diagnostically because of this criterion. He cites an analysis by the National Data Bank for Rheumatic Diseases that found that 84% of people could accurately be diagnosed with FM when fatigue, regional pain, the number of somatic symptoms, and the number of lifetime comorbid illnesses, rather than tender points, are taken into consideration. Wolfe now urges that the 1990 criteria should stop being used. Despite his urging, the criteria continue to be used today.

The debate about the "realness" of FM is not necessarily a moot point. Many hypotheses concerning psychosocial factors that are suspected to play a role in FM have not been tested. This presents many research opportunities to determine the extent that factors such as societal "grooming" of susceptible people, positive social gains such as disability compensation, and excessive stresses of modern westernized life play in FM. For example, Canadian physicians Kevin P. White and John Thompson addressed these factors in their 2003 epidemiological study.

They examined the prevalence of fibromyalgia symptoms in an Amish group (number = 179) in comparison with its prevalence in a non-Amish rural group (control

FAST FACT

A controversial, experimental treatment for fibromyalgia involves Mucinex or other guaifenesin drugs typically used to break up mucus in a patient's airway. Those who prescribe this treatment option believe fibromyalgia results from calcium phosphate deposits, but a patient study has contradicted that hypothesis.

group 1; n = 492) and its prevalence in an urban group (control group 2; n = 3,395). White and Thompson specifically chose Amish subjects since this society does not have disability compensation for its disabled members, the Amish have a strong work ethic, and Amish life does not have the fast-paced stresses typical of modern life. With this in mind, the researchers expected that the prevalence of FM symptoms would be nonexistent or nearly so. They found that 7.3% of the Amish subjects, 1.2% of the non-Amish rural, and 3.8% of the urban subjects had FM symptoms. Although White and Thompson were surprised that the Amish had a higher prevalence of FM symptoms than urban or non-Amish rural, they concluded that factors such as societal "grooming," disability compensation, or stresses associated with a fast-paced life could not be playing a role in FM. Although only briefly mentioned in their study, White and Thompson believe that the high prevalence of FM in the Amish society may point to the impact of genetics in FM. (The Amish have a high rate of inbreeding.) They encourage more FM studies to be done among the Amish to examine this issue.

FM and Sleep

Diagnosing FM and therefore treating it can be problematic. One reason for the diagnostic difficulty is that FM shares many symptoms in common with other disorders. For example, hypocalcemia (low blood calcium level) and low vitamin-D level can result in muscle soreness and tenderness; hypothyroidism can result in fatigue; and infections such as Lyme disease and arthritis can result in pain that is similar to fibromyalgia. However, these disorders can be more easily ruled out through testing. There is no definitive test for FM. Therefore, FM is currently diagnosed after other disorders have been ruled out and if a person meets the two 1990 FM criteria. Adding to the difficulty, FM sufferers may also have nonpain complaints

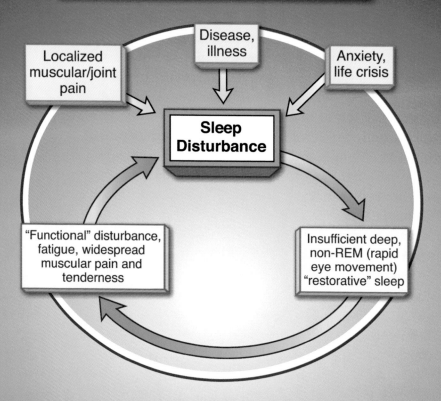

The Cycle of Pain and Sleep Disturbance in Fibromyalgia

Localized muscular/joint pain

Disease, illness

Anxiety, life crisis

Sleep Disturbance

Insufficient deep, non-REM (rapid eye movement) "restorative" sleep

"Functional" disturbance, fatigue, widespread muscular pain and tenderness

Taken from: Byers Chiropractic Center, copyright Chiromatrix.™
www.drjmbyers.com/custom_contact/27844_fibromyalgia.html.

such as gastrointestinal problems (eg, irritable bowel–like symptoms, nausea), mood disorders (eg, depression), and sleep disturbances (eg, insomnia, restless legs syndrome).

Treating an FM patient often involves treating a variety of symptoms, primarily pain. Pain medications often do not work for long or at all in reducing the pain. Pregabalin is the first that appears to be able to reduce pain in clinical studies. Scientists are not sure of the mechanism by which it does this. They believe that it binds to hyperexcited neurons responsible for pain perception in the brain, and induces the neurons to slow their firing. Studies also indicate that pregabalin improves sleep. People taking the drug have fewer arousals from sleep and increased amounts of slow wave sleep.

The impact of pregabalin on sleep may be beneficial, since there is a high prevalence of sleep disorders in people with FM. Some common sleep disorders found in FM sufferers are insomnia, restless legs syndrome/periodic leg movement disorder (RLS/PLMD), and sleep apnea. RLS/PLMD and sleep apnea are primary sleep disorders (disorders having no other cause), but insomnia is often a secondary sleep disorder (caused by another disorder). It is commonly thought that pain causes insomnia in people with FM. However, some studies indicate that insomnia may not result from FM pain; instead, FM may be a manifestation of an intrinsic sleep disorder that disrupts sleep, which in turn plays a role in pain.

In 1975, [researchers Harvey] Moldofsky et al noted that people deprived of delta sleep (slow wave sleep) experienced physical symptoms very similar to those experienced by people with fibromyalgia. The researchers induced a slight arousal in healthy subjects just as the subjects were about to enter stage 4 sleep (sleep comprised of 50% or more delta waves on an electroencephalogram [EEG]). After 3 nights of stage 4 sleep deprivation, the subjects complained of "heaviness" of the entire body, somatic fatigue, and mood changes such as depression and irritability. Some subjects also complained of loss of appetite or gastrointestinal complaints such as nausea and diarrhea. Additionally, Moldofsky et al noted that on each successive night of stage 4 sleep deprivation, it became harder to arouse the subject from sleep; when they were able to induce an arousal, the person had mixed alpha and delta waves on the EEG for a period of up to 20 seconds. (People with FM frequently have alpha-delta sleep.) From these findings, Moldofsky et al proposed that FM may be a "nonrestorative sleep syndrome." That is, rather than pain disrupting sleep, FM may be a symptom of an arousal dysfunction that disrupts sleep and results in pain and other symptoms of FM.

Other scientists are not convinced that FM is an intrinsic sleep disorder. Drs Maren L. and Mark W. Mahowald point out that other sleep disorders such as obstructive sleep apnea (OSA), which can drastically disrupt sleep, do not result in the muscular problems noted in FM.

Treating Sleep Disorder May Help FM

Nevertheless, treating sleep disorders in people with FM may help improve symptoms by improving sleep quality. Cognitive behavior therapy or other behavioral approaches aimed at improving sleep hygiene, fitness, and proper nutrition can help stabilize the sleep-wake rhythms in a person with FM. Hypnotic drugs may help a person initiate and maintain sleep, thereby reducing daytime sleepiness. Tricyclic drugs such as amitriptyline and cyclobenzaprine can result in long-term improved sleep.

Primary care physicians often overlook the impact of poor sleep quality on symptoms in their FM patients, especially if the person complains only of pain. However, treating sleep disorders in people with FM may have a beneficial effect on FM symptoms by preventing arousals during sleep. More consolidated sleep means less disrupted slow wave sleep and improved physical restoration. Therefore, a physician may need to ask an FM patient questions about symptoms of a sleep disorder such as loud snoring or sensations of choking during sleep (symptoms of OSA); annoying crawling sensations before going to sleep (RLS); awakening with leg cramps (PLMD); or difficulty initiating or maintaining sleep (insomnia). Effective care for an FM patient often involves many facets. For some FM patients, improved sleep may need to be one of the facets of care.

CHAPTER 2

Controversies Concerning Fibromyalgia

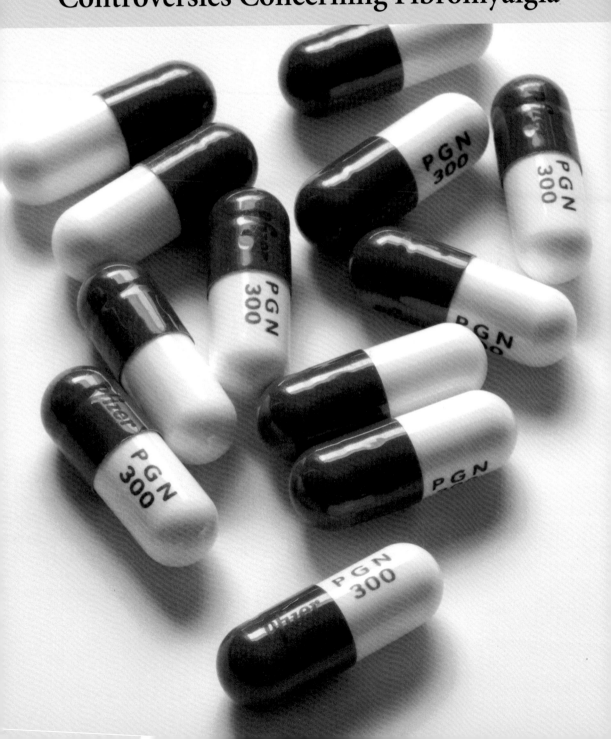

Pharmaceutical Companies Are Hyping Fibromyalgia in Order to Sell Drugs

Matthew Perrone

In the following article Matthew Perrone points out that drugmakers spent hundreds of millions of dollars in 2008 to raise awareness about fibromyalgia, which some experts believe is not even a "real" disease. According to Perrone, much of the money was donated to nonprofit organizations and educational campaigns. The author says that many doctors and patients believe that this was legitimate education of doctors about an illness that has been misunderstood, but critics say the companies engaged in disease-mongering merely to get people to use their drugs. Whatever their motive, the effort paid off, as sales of the drugs recently approved for fibromyalgia rose dramatically from 2007 to 2008—to over $700 million for Lyrica alone. Perrone is a journalist with the Associated Press.

Photo on previous page. Lyrica is just one of the latest drugs designed to treat fibromyalgia. (Chris Gallagher/Photo Researchers, Inc.)

Two drugmakers spent hundreds of millions of dollars last year to raise awareness of a murky illness, helping boost sales of pills recently approved as treatments and

SOURCE: Matthew Perrone, "Disease May Not Be Real, but the Drug Profits Are," *Houston Chronicle* (Associated Press), February 8, 2009. Reprinted with permission of the Associated Press.

drowning out unresolved questions—including whether it's a real disease at all.

Key components of the industry-funded buzz over the pain-and-fatigue ailment fibromyalgia are grants—more than $6 million donated by drugmakers Eli Lilly and Pfizer in the first three quarters of 2008—to nonprofit groups for medical conferences and educational campaigns, an Associated Press analysis found.

That's more than they gave for more accepted ailments, such as diabetes and Alzheimer's. Among grants tied to specific diseases, fibromyalgia ranked third for each company, behind only cancer and AIDS for Pfizer and cancer and depression for Lilly.

Fibromyalgia draws skepticism for several reasons. The cause is unknown. There are no tests to confirm a diagnosis. Many patients also fit the criteria for chronic fatigue syndrome and other pain ailments.

> **FAST FACT**
>
> In June 2009 Data-monitor, a provider of business information, forecast that the fibromyalgia market will more than double in value from 2008 to total $2.5 billion world-wide by 2018.

Experts don't doubt the patients are in pain. They differ on what to call it and how to treat it.

Awareness or Hype?

Many doctors and patients say the drugmakers are educating the medical establishment about a misunderstood illness, much as they did with depression in the 1980s. Those with fibromyalgia have often had to fight perceptions that they are hypochondriacs, or even faking their pain.

But critics say the companies are hyping fibromyalgia along with their treatments, and that the grant-making is a textbook example of how drugmakers unduly influence doctors and patients.

"I think the purpose of most pharmaceutical company efforts is to do a little disease-mongering and to have people

Dr. Frederick Wolfe, a leading fibromyalgia researcher, believes that drug companies are too quick to market drugs as remedies for an affliction that is not yet clearly understood. (**AP Images**)

use their drugs," said Dr. Frederick Wolfe, who was lead author of the guidelines defining fibromyalgia in 1990 but has since become one of its leading skeptics.

Drug Sales Multiply

Whatever the motive, the push has paid off. Between the first quarter of 2007 and the fourth quarter of 2008, sales rose from $395 million to $702 million for Pfizer's Lyrica, and $442 million to $721 million for Lilly's Cymbalta.

Cymbalta, an antidepressant, won Food and Drug Administration approval as a treatment for fibromyalgia in June. Lyrica, originally approved for epileptic seizures, was approved for fibromyalgia a year earlier.

Drugmakers respond to skepticism by pointing out that fibromyalgia is recognized by medical societies, including the American College of Rheumatology.

"I think what we're seeing here is just the evolution of greater awareness about a condition that has generally been neglected or poorly managed," said Steve Romano, a Pfizer vice president who oversees its neuroscience division.

The FDA approved the drugs because they've been shown to reduce pain in fibromyalgia patients, though it's not clear how.

Side effects include nausea, weight gain and drowsiness.

"I call it my fibromyalgia fog, because I'm so medicated I go through the day feeling like I'm not really there," said Helen Arellanes of Los Angeles. She takes five medications for pain, including Lyrica and Cymbalta.

The Debate on Fibromyalgia

Pfizer and Eli Lilly are promoting drugs to treat fibromyalgia, an ailment characterized by pain, fatigue and depression. But some doctors say the marketing buzz is drowning out important questions about the condition, including:

- *The cause.* There is still no agreement on that, though some scientists point to abnormalities in the nervous system.
- *The test.* Unlike other pain conditions, such as arthritis, there is no medical test for fibromyalgia. Instead, doctors make a diagnosis by examining patients and considering symptoms.
- *Unique.* A quarter of patients diagnosed also fit the criteria of other disorders, raising questions about whether this is a unique disease.

Where People with Fibromyalgia Obtain Information

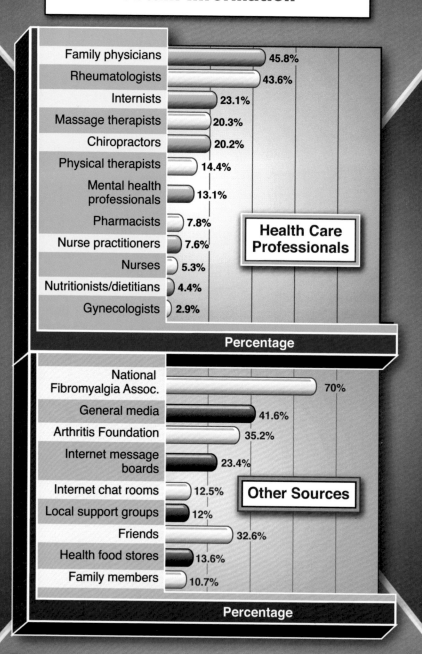

Health Care Professionals

Family physicians	45.8%
Rheumatologists	43.6%
Internists	23.1%
Massage therapists	20.3%
Chiropractors	20.2%
Physical therapists	14.4%
Mental health professionals	13.1%
Pharmacists	7.8%
Nurse practitioners	7.6%
Nurses	5.3%
Nutritionists/dietitians	4.4%
Gynecologists	2.9%

Percentage

Other Sources

National Fibromyalgia Assoc.	70%
General media	41.6%
Arthritis Foundation	35.2%
Internet message boards	23.4%
Internet chat rooms	12.5%
Local support groups	12%
Friends	32.6%
Health food stores	13.6%
Family members	10.7%

Percentage

These results are based on a survey of 2,596 people who visited the National Fibromyalgia Association Web site.

Taken from: Robert M Bennet et al., "An Internet Survey of 2,596 People with Fibromyalgia," *BioMed Central Journal of Musculoskeletal Disorders*, March 9, 2007. www.biomedcentral.com/1471-2474/8/27.

- *Mind over matter.* Patients are more likely to have a history of mental illness, be overweight and economically disadvantaged. Some doctors say their suffering may stem from difficult circumstances rather than disease.

Lyrica Helps Patients Whether They Do or Do Not Have Psychological Problems

Medical News Today

The following article discusses the results of combined studies of over two thousand fibromyalgia patients to analyze the effectiveness of the drug Lyrica, originally intended to treat depression. According to Medical News Today, researchers found that it was significantly more effective than a placebo (an inactive substance such as a sugar pill that the patient believes is a drug) in reducing pain and improving sleep. The improvement in fatigue, anxiety, and depression was less, but still statistically significant. Furthermore, claims the author, the drug helped reduce pain regardless of whether a patient was anxious or depressed, which was considered important. However, Lyrica can cause serious allergic reactions as well as side effects such as dizziness, weight gain, and blurred vision, among others, so it is not good for everyone. Medical News Today is an independent health and medical news Web site with articles, videos, and forums.

SOURCE: Medical News Today, "Lyrica Reduced Pain of Fibromyalgia in Patients Regardless of Symptoms of Anxiety or Depression." www.medicalnewstoday.com, April 18, 2008. Reproduced by permission.

Pfizer's Lyrica reduced pain of fibromyalgia in patients regardless of whether they experienced symptoms of anxiety or depression at the beginning of the study, according to a pooled analysis presented today [in April 2008] at the American Academy of Neurology annual meeting. The analysis, which looked at data pooled from previous clinical trials, also showed that patients' self-reported improvements were more closely associated with improvements in pain and sleep than with improvements in fatigue or symptoms of anxiety or depression.

Fibromyalgia is the most common, chronic widespread pain condition in the United States and is thought to result from neurological changes in how patients perceive pain. Fibromyalgia is usually accompanied by poor sleep, stiffness and fatigue.

> **FAST FACT**
>
> As of 2009, the U.S. Food and Drug Administration had approved three drugs to treat fibromyalgia. Their brand names are Lyrica, Cymbalta, and Savella.

"The data showed that Lyrica reduced fibromyalgia pain, and alleviating that pain was associated with patients' overall feeling of well-being," said Dr. Lesley Arnold, one of the study's authors and associate professor in the department of psychiatry at the University of Cincinnati Medical Center. "Understandably, many patients with a chronic pain condition such as fibromyalgia also experience depression and anxiety, and importantly we found that Lyrica helped reduce pain in patients regardless of the presence of symptoms of these co-morbid conditions."

About the Analysis

The results are from a retrospective, pooled analysis of data from three placebo-controlled clinical trials (8 weeks, 13 weeks and 14 weeks long) of Lyrica in over 2,000 fibromyalgia patients. These studies randomized patients to receive Lyrica 150 mg, 300 mg, 450 mg or 600 mg or

Patient Response to Lyrica in Fibromyalgia Study

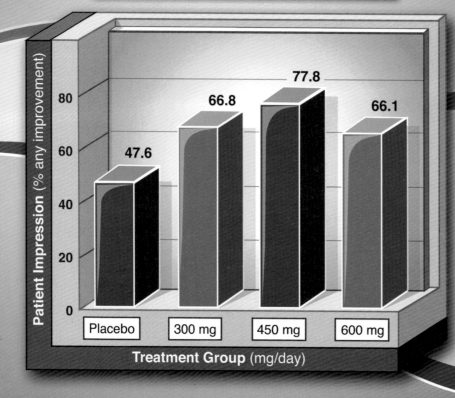

Patient Impression (% any improvement)

47.6

66.8

77.8

66.1

Placebo | 300 mg | 450 mg | 600 mg

Treatment Group (mg/day)

Taken from: Pfizer, "Full Prescribing Information for Lyrica." www.pfizer.com/files/products/uspi_lyrica.pdf.

placebo. Patients were asked to measure their pain on a scale of zero to 10; the baseline score for study participants was 6.9 (150 mg, 450 mg, 600 mg) or 7.0 (300 mg). A score of 4.0 to 6.9 is considered moderate pain and a score of greater than 7.0 is considered moderate to severe pain on this 10-point scale.

In the studies, 38 percent of fibromyalgia patients had moderate to severe anxiety symptoms, while 27 percent had moderate to severe depressive symptoms, as assessed using the Hospital Anxiety and Depression Scales (HADS-A or HADS-D). Patients with severe depression or unstable psychiatric conditions were excluded from the studies.

The new analysis confirmed that Lyrica was significantly more effective than placebo in reducing pain in patients with fibromyalgia. Patients receiving 600 mg a day of Lyrica had a pain reduction of 2.08 on the pain scale; 450 mg a day had a reduction of 2.01; 300 mg a day had a reduction of 1.76; 150 mg a day had a reduction of 1.37, and placebo had a reduction of 1.25. Additionally, Lyrica was found to reduce pain in patients regardless of whether they had symptoms of anxiety or depression.

The analysis also examined the relationship between improvements in pain, sleep, fatigue, anxiety and depressive symptoms with patients reporting feeling "much improved" or "very much improved" as measured by the Patient Global Impression of Change (PGIC). The PGIC is a standardized, self-reported tool that measures the change in a patient's overall status ranging from "very much improved" to "very much worse."

Pain reduction was found to have the greatest association on patients reporting improvement as measured by PGIC. The relationships between feeling much or very much improved were strongest for pain and sleep, and less pronounced for fatigue and symptoms of anxiety or depression, but statistically significant for all variables.

The most common side effects in the pooled analysis versus placebo of these three studies were dizziness and somnolence, followed by weight gain, blurred vision and dry mouth.

Lyrica Has Advantages and Possible Side Effects

In the United States, Lyrica® (pregabalin) capsules, CV, is approved for the management of fibromyalgia. Lyrica is also indicated for the management of neuropathic pain

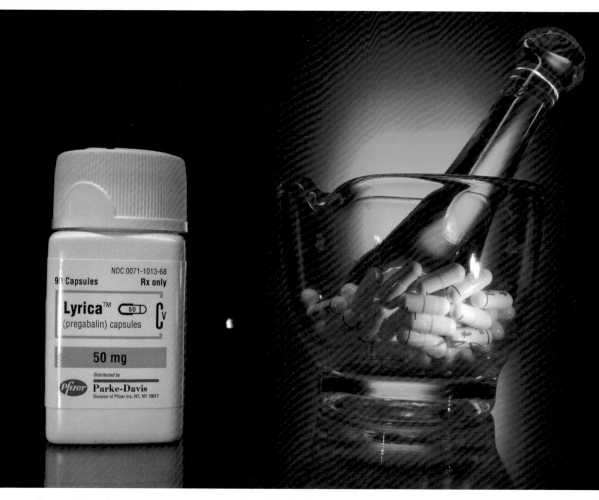

Researchers have found the drug Lyrica to be effective in reducing pain and improving sleep in some fibromyalgia patients.
(Bloomberg/Bloomberg via Getty Images)

associated with diabetic peripheral neuropathy, postherpetic neuralgia (pain after shingles), and as adjunctive therapy for adults with partial onset seizures. The 600 mg/day is not an approved dosage for Lyrica in the management of fibromyalgia.

Lyrica is not for everyone. Lyrica may cause serious allergic reactions. Patients should tell their doctors right away about any serious allergic reaction such as swelling of the face, mouth, lips, gums, tongue or neck or if they have any trouble breathing. Other allergic reactions may include rash, hives and blisters. Patients should tell their doctors about any changes in eyesight, including blurry vision, muscle pain along with a fever or tired feeling, or skin sores due to diabetes.

Some of the most common side effects of Lyrica are dizziness, sleepiness, weight gain, blurred vision, dry mouth, feeling "high," swelling of hands and feet, and trouble concentrating. Patients may have a higher chance for swelling and hives if they are also taking angiotensin converting enzyme (ACE) inhibitors so they should let their doctors know if they are taking these medications. They may have a higher chance of swelling or gaining weight if they are also taking certain diabetes medicines.

Patients should not drive a car or operate machinery until they know how Lyrica affects them. Patients should not drink alcohol while on Lyrica. Patients should be especially careful about medicines that make them sleepy and should also tell their doctors if they are planning to father a child. Patients should tell their doctor if they are pregnant, plan to become pregnant, or are breast-feeding. If they have had a drug or alcohol problem, they may be more likely to misuse Lyrica. Patients should talk with their doctor before they stop taking Lyrica, or any other prescription medication. Lyrica is one of several treatment options for doctors to consider.

The Act of Treating Fibromyalgia May Make Patients Worse

Nortin M. Hadler

In the following viewpoint Nortin M. Hadler, a noted critic of the belief that fibromyalgia has a physical cause, argues that people with persistent widespread pain lack the ability to cope with the stress of life as well as other people do. He does not mean that their physical pain is not real, but he believes the underlying reason for it is psychological and that focusing on it, labeling it a disease, and searching for a physical cure make it worse and prevent recovery. This is especially true, he says, when the patient must prove to the doctor, or to others, that he or she is sick. Hadler is a professor of medicine at the University of North Carolina and an attending rheumatologist at University of North Carolina hospitals.

If questioned closely, nearly all of us can recall low-back pain in the last year. A third of us can recall pain at the shoulder, and nearly as many can recall pain at

SOURCE: Nortin M. Hadler, *The Last Well Person: How to Stay Well Despite the Health-Care System.* Montreal, QC: McGill-Queen's University Press, 2004. Copyright © 2004 McGill-Queen's University Press. Reproduced by permission.

the hand, elbow, or wrist that lasted at least a week. Regional musculoskeletal pain is but one of the intermittent and remittent predicaments of normal life. Feeling "well" demands the sense of invincibility that we can cope with our next musculoskeletal or other symptoms. Being "well" means that we had the wherewithal to cope with the last challenge so effectively that it is barely a memory, if at all. It does not mean avoiding these challenges, for heartache, heartburn, headache, and all the other aches are part of life.

I emphasize regional musculoskeletal disorders here because they are the chief complaint of a sizable minority of people who seek the ministrations of primary care physicians and of the vast majority who consult chiropractors and other practitioners of manual medicine. . . .

The narrative of distress of a patient with a regional musculoskeletal disorder is often delivered as a substitute for difficulties the person is having in coping with the demands of life that render the musculoskeletal disorder the last straw. "My back hurts" may well mean "My back hurts, but I'm here because I can't cope with this episode," or, more particularly, ". . . because I can't cope with this episode as well as the turmoil at home (or work)." Yet treatment acts for back pain are wont to focus exclusively on the back. The same can be said of treatment acts for shoulder pain focusing on the shoulder, knee pain on the knee, and so on. Such is the patient's expectation in seeking care, and the expertise purveyed by the chosen professional. The clinical contract demands specific treatment for the cause of the pain. Yet for nearly all the regional musculoskeletal disorders, such a treatment act rests on the shakiest of scientific groups. . . .

I suspect these treatment acts don't work because they focus on the pathoanatomy, and not the psychosocial confounders to coping. To resort to cliché, they miss the forest for the trees. Regardless of the fact that these treatment acts do not work, the patient is instructed on the various clinical hypotheses on which the treatments are based. Needless to say, such instruction will irretrievably alter the patient's conception of his own health, as well as the general choice of idioms to describe current and future distress.

Persistent Widespread Pain

Hidden in all the community surveys of people with discrete regional musculoskeletal disorders are individuals burdened with persistent pain at multiple sites. Their numbers are impressive, varying between 3 and 10 per cent of the population, depending on the definition used and the community studied, but only recently has their plight been recognized. People with regional musculoskeletal pain at multiple sites are more likely to manifest psychological disturbance and to report other physical, or somatic, symptoms than people who suffer from, or recall, discrete regional disorders. They are frequent consumers of medical care. These individuals are often bedevilled by so many life challenges that any quest for some sense of being well, let alone of invincibility, is doomed. The intermittent and remittent morbid predicaments of life that well people find surmountable are insufferable and unforgettable setbacks for those living under this pall. Hence, they take note of and report other somatic symptoms. Variation in bowel habits looms large, and diminished vigour oppresses them. *Joie de vivre* [enjoyment of life] is absent.

I suspect that few people suffering with persistent chronic pain suffer in silence. I further suspect that their narrative of distress depends on the listener. The idioms of distress that enlist the empathy of a clergyman are not the same as those that enhance communication with a social worker, a sibling, or a physician. We have no data on how these unhappy people select a confidant, but their cultural setting is likely to influence this decision. If they are seduced by the blandishment of "scientific" or pseudo-

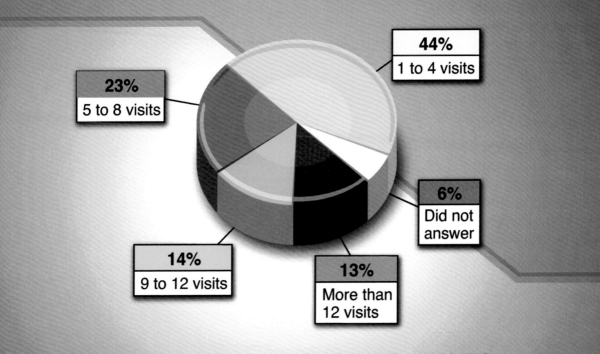

Frequency of Fibromyalgia Patients' Visits to Health Care Providers During One Year

44%
1 to 4 visits

23%
5 to 8 visits

6%
Did not answer

14%
9 to 12 visits

13%
More than 12 visits

Taken from: Robert M. Bennett et al., "An Internet Survey of 2,596 People with Fibromyalgia," *BioMed Central Journal of Musculoskeletal Disorders*, March 9, 2007. www.biomedcentral.com/1471-2474/8/27.

scientific medicine, they will choose a physician or some other health practitioner. As we have seen, the medical contract demands specific treatment for the cause of the pain, though the treatment provided, seemingly rational or not, is unlikely to have a scientific grounding. Such supposedly scientific treatment acts abound, generally predicated on a circularity of argument. The symptoms are ranked, a specific pathology is postulated, and a neologic diagnostic label is applied that reiterates the presenting symptoms. . . .

The Mistaken Identity Attached to "Fibromyalgia"

This sequence of events shows how individuals suffering persistent widespread pain learn to be patients with "fibromyalgia." The clinician can find no specific cause for the complaint of persistent widespread pain but feels compelled to discern that the patient dislikes being poked at particular bodily sites. Since fibromyalgia is defined as a state of chronic widespread pain and tenderness at certain points, the clinician pronounces, "You have fibromyalgia." Any clinician who applies the fibromyalgia label and promulgates a treatment act on that basis must disregard the observation that putatively diagnostic "tender points" are related to generalized pain and pain behaviour. Fibromyalgia denotes nothing more than persistent widespread pain. However, in the labelling, the patient is forever changed. . . .

Critics of fibromyalgia treatments say that although some doctors attempt to treat patients' physical pain—which is real—the underlying causes may be psychological rather than physical. (© Nic Cleave/Alamy)

The proponents of the fibromyalgia construction are convinced that their pathophysiological insights and theories are valid, though as yet unproved, and their therapeutic approaches need but tweaking to produce the benefits that have eluded demonstration to date. They could, of course, be right, but, undoubtedly, their approach is causing harm today. I admit it is possible that a therapeutic triumph is but one scientific discovery away, rendering my psychosocial and sociocultural synthesis secondary, if not fatuous. After all, it would not have been far fetched to have constructed sociocultural models for the pathogenesis of pulmonary tuberculosis and AIDS were it not for the superseding microbiology. Many an intrepid investigator has stalked the cause of fibromyalgia in the labyrinth of our neuroendocrine and immune systems for just that reason, but clues are hard to come by, and subtle changes prove unreliable secondary, or non-specific....

Life Under a Pall

I am suggesting that chronic persistent pain is an ideation, or somatization, engendered in response to the living of life under a pall, and not vice versa. I am not defining "pall" further because my theory countenances a wide range of individual differences in this tendency to somatize. These unfortunate people choose to be patients because they have exhausted their wherewithal to cope. If this suggestion is correct, the complaint of persistent widespread pain should initiate a treatment act quite different from that leading to labelling as fibromyalgia. The symptoms of persistent widespread pain should be heard as probable surrogate complaints for difficulties in coping with life's sometimes overwhelming problems. Months, often years, of poking, testing, pharmaceutical products, and medicalization might be avoided by directly approaching the coping challenge....

The people in the community who are burdened by persistent widespread pain, but have yet to avail themselves of a treatment act that labels them with fibromyalgia, suffer more than just chronic pervasive pain. Other everyday symptoms become momentous for them. Unlike the invincible person, people who are succumbing to the challenges of life and who use illness as a surrogate complaint seem to accumulate a host of unpleasant and unexpected bodily events. It appears that something must be dreadfully wrong. Some of these people quietly accept this sad state as their lot, but others vigorously cast about for an answer. The lay press and the Internet are at their service, as are many health-care professionals. . . .

To me, another approach is to say that these people are predisposed to somatize when they are under stress, and this predisposition takes over their lives when they are overwhelmed by life's difficulties. Unfortunately, they are then rendered only more ill by the process of medicalization.

All of us somatize to some degree. . . . On such occasions we feel "blue," or become aware of our bowels, or feel tired or stiff as if we have slept poorly. Sometime we know why, for challenges at home or at work are all too obvious. If we are concerned that our aggravating knee pain or backache or headache has returned, or is worse and harder to bear, we become even more out of sorts. Sometimes there is no known association—it just happens. Fortunately, it just passes, too. A bit of good news, a beautiful day, or an invigorating walk is often salving. . . .

If You Have to Prove You Are Ill, You Cannot Get Well

Some circumstances in life predispose most, if not all, of us to somatize and catastrophize. Abusive relationships, job dissatisfaction, and job insecurity will do it, as will a worker's compensation claim for a chronically disabling regional musculoskeletal disorder (back pain, arm pain, or fibromyalgia in particular). . . .

Patients labelled with fibromyalgia are, by definition, spared any coincidental demonstrable specific damage. These people have to prove their illness in the absence of disease. The only way to do so depends on emotion and body language, levels of communication foreign to bureaucracies. The inevitable contest may be broached by the health insurer, who must approve treatment, or, more often, by an insurance carrier who needs to determine the magnitude of disability consequent to the fibromyalgia. . . .

The patient with the pervasive illness labelled fibromyalgia will get sicker and less capable of performing in society. That patient will focus on all the symptoms, recalling and often recording them at the instruction of legal counsel in a drive to document the magnitude of the illness. Symptom magnification is predictable. Since the veracity of the symptoms is at stake, any diminution in their intensity is made virtually impossible. Regression in intensity is tantamount to yielding to the insinuations that the symptoms were feigned in the first place. Illness escalates predictably. The other predictable outcome is that considerable wealth will be transferred from those who pay premiums to all those involved in this medicolegal process—with the exception, often, of the claimant, for whom pathos is the reward, and impoverishment the price to be paid.

The contest I've outlined plays out in a public arena. A more private contest awaits the person with persistent widespread pain who chooses to seek medical recourse. While less violent than the medicolegal contest, it is as likely to inflame the illness. This contest begins when the physician and the patient set out to define the biological "cause" of the persistent widespread pain as a prerequisite to treatment—a process that is bound to recruit the patient's undivided

> **FAST FACT**
>
> Difficulty in concentrating or remembering—a condition patients often call "fibro fog"—is common in fibromyalgia. However, by no means do all fibromyalgia patients have such problems; in many cases the symptoms are entirely physical.

attention. The persistent widespread pain is then medicalized. The contest remains subliminal until the diagnostic process has proven fruitless, a time-consuming and anxiety-provoking exercise in testing, consulting, and running down false clues. The diminishing return of the diagnostic exercise is met with increasing tension in the patient-physician interaction. Any suggestions the doctor now offers about the value of psychological counselling are heard as accusations of the diagnosis "it's in your mind." The patient is placed in the position of proving to the physician that the pain is real—and proving the same to sceptics in the family, the social network, and the workplace. Such patients often recall and record symptoms in the course of the treatment act, just as they do in the course of a more public litigious contest. Their illness escalates. For these patients, caught in this vortex, the label fibromyalgia is much more than a diagnosis; it becomes a symbol of self-actualization. For me, or anyone else, to discuss its semiotics or to offer a sociocultural theory of pathogenesis is infuriating. That, too, is viewed as an assault on their veracity, an accusation that their symptoms are "in their mind."

Patients with Fibromyalgia May Have Central Nervous System Abnormalities

Christine Kilgore

In the following article Christine Kilgore reports that a large amount of data now suggests that the central nervous systems of patients with fibromyalgia work differently from the average and that real differences exist in the way their brains process pain. Most studies of fibromyalgia are small, says the author, but reviewing many of them yields a consistent picture of an underlying neurobiological basis for the disorder. According to Kilgore, evidence seems to suggest that fibromyalgia is a manifestation of an abnormal acute stress response involving hormones, among other factors. Furthermore, she asserts, some recent studies have shown that close relatives of patients have the same sort of unusual sensitivity to pain. Kilgore is a medical writer and editor based in Washington, D.C.

SOURCE: Christine Kilgore, "Overactive CNS Processing Tied to Fibromyalgia: When Viewed Together, Neuroimaging Studies Show Strong Neurobiologic Underpinnings of Disorder," *Clinical Psychiatry News*, vol. 35, March 2007, p. 34. Copyright © 2007 International Medical News Group. Reproduced by permission.

An "overwhelming" amount of data now suggest that patients with fibromyalgia and a number of overlapping pain syndromes have augmented pain or sensory processing in the central nervous system [CNS], resulting in real differences in pain tolerance, judging from the findings of a recent review.

Genetic findings also are accumulating that suggest specific gene mutations may predispose individuals to developing fibromyalgia (FM), according to the authors.

"It is time for us to move past the rhetoric about whether these conditions are real, and take these patients seriously as we endeavor to learn more about the causes and most effective treatments for these disorders," reported Dr. Daniel J. Clauw, professor of rheumatology at the University of Michigan [U-M], Ann Arbor, and director of the U-M Chronic Pain and Fatigue Research Center, and Richard E. Harris, Ph.D., a researcher at the center and the university.

The hyperactivity of pain processing mechanisms that characterizes FM and related conditions—from irritable bowel syndrome to tension headache and temporomandibular syndrome—can occur in association with psychological factors, "but psychological factors are not in any way required for an individual to develop or maintain this augmented central pain state," they wrote.

Other investigators said in an interview that they hope to see more reviews like it, particularly since many studies of FM are low budget, small and too easily dismissed unless they are viewed together.

Small Studies Must Be Viewed Together

Neuroimaging studies, for instance, "are providing a consistent picture" when viewed together of strong neurobiologic underpinnings for FM, said Dr. Nancy Klimas, professor of medicine at the University of Miami. "But if you pull them apart, you can find faults with any one

Possible Neurological Connections to Fibromyalgia Symptoms

If, as some suggest, fibromyalgia patients have central nervous system abnormalities, the ways in which their brain circuits function and their hormones are regulated may explain their heightened sensitivity to pain and an array of other symptoms associated with the syndrome.

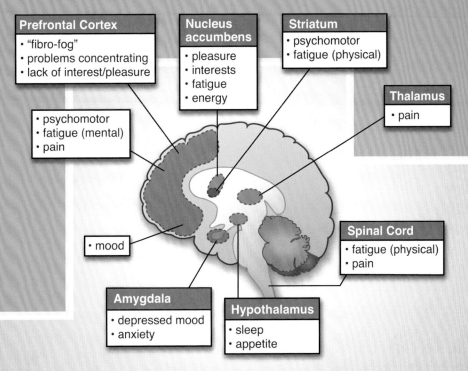

Prefrontal Cortex
• "fibro-fog"
• problems concentrating
• lack of interest/pleasure

Nucleus accumbens
• pleasure
• interests
• fatigue
• energy

Striatum
• psychomotor
• fatigue (physical)

Thalamus
• pain

• psychomotor
• fatigue (mental)
• pain

• mood

Spinal Cord
• fatigue (physical)
• pain

Amygdala
• depressed mood
• anxiety

Hypothalamus
• sleep
• appetite

Taken from: Stephen M. Stahl, "Chapter 15: Pain and the Treatment of Fibromyalgia and Functional Somatic Syndromes," *Stahl's Essential Psychopharmacology Online*, 3rd ed., 2008. http://stahlonline.cambridge.org/common_home.jsf.

study in it having limited power, or some other limitation."

"This is what [the authors] are saying—'look at the whole picture, it's impressive,'" said Dr. Klimas. "There's some real science to go behind the pain observation."

Dr. Klimas said the review reminded her of a grand-rounds lecture she heard several years ago, in which a "prominent" department chair told students and faculty that fibromyalgia "is all in patients' heads."

"He essentially said, don't let these patients talk to each other, don't let them read anything, don't let them have any support group meetings," Dr. Klimas said. "I was livid. These patients [with FM] are often treated badly by their physicians. It's bad enough leaving without any hope that something can be done, but it's worse leaving a doctor's office having been made to feel small or patronized."

Dr. Laurence Bradley, professor of medicine in the division of clinical immunology and rheumatology at the University of Alabama, agreed that the literature is ripe for strong conclusions. "The [review authors] are correct. A lot of new findings have emerged in the last 5–8 years . . . regarding gene variance that's associated with FM itself or with [related] disorders. And a lot of the neuroimaging work that has been done has demonstrated very convincingly that people with FM have enhanced or abnormal transmission of sensory signals through the CNS," he said. "Behavioral studies —laboratory pain studies—also show consistent displays of abnormal pain responses in individuals with FM."

In their review, Dr. Clauw and Dr. Harris described functional imaging studies done with single-photon emission computer tomography (SPECT) and functional magnetic resonance imaging (fMRI) that show differences in neural activation between patients with FM and pain-free controls. The studies indicate that FM patients have abnormalities within their central brain structures, they said. There is evidence in FM that an "increased gain" in pain processing is driven by defects in both descending inhibitory pathways for pain processing and in spinal excitatory activity, the authors added. . . .

FAST FACT

Research done by psychiatry professor Lesley Arnold, cited by rheumatologist Daniel Clauw in a *New York Times* interview, found that relatives of people with fibromyalgia were eight times more likely to have it than family members of people without the disorder. This suggests that it is at least partially genetic.

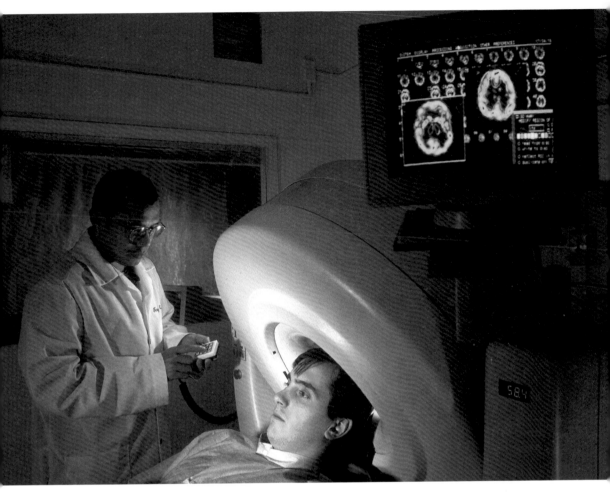

Trials Show That Drugs Used for Neuropathic Pain Also Help Fibromyalgia

The "ultimate proof" that defective central control mechanisms are playing a role in FM and overlapping pain conditions comes from randomized clinical trials showing that neuroactive compounds that either increase inhibitory activity (such as serotonin-norepinephrine reuptake inhibitors) or decrease facilitatory activity (such as antiepileptics) can be efficacious in treating FM as well as neuropathic pain, said Dr. Clauw and Dr. Harris.

A subject participating in fibromyalgia research undergoes a SPECT scan, an imaging technique used in diagnosing abnormalities within the central brain structure. (Richard T. Nowitz/Photo Researchers, Inc.)

Dr. Bradley said that one of the "missing pieces of information" in the growing knowledge of pain transmission in FM is its original source. "Where's the starting point?" he asked. "[Many experts] think it originates from abnormalities in the deep muscle tissue, but at this point we have a much better understanding of what goes on at the spinal level than we do of what factors contribute to the initiation of sensory signals."

What's missing from the review itself, he and others noted, is the "consistent" evidence of altered neuroendocrine function in patients with FM.

Dr. Robert Bennett, who has led studies in this area, said that FM also appears to be a manifestation of an abnormal acute stress response involving abnormalities in levels of cortisol and growth hormone, an imbalance in sympathetic and vagal tone, and other phenomena—a notion that puts FM at least partly in the same camp, for underlying mechanisms, as chronic fatigue syndrome.

"The major things we know now [about FM] relate to the pain system," said Dr. Bennett, professor of medicine at Oregon Health and Science University, Portland. "The neuroendocrine abnormalities—the manifestations of the acute stress response—have still, I think, been underinvestigated."

Dr. Klimas, director of the University of Miami's chronic fatigue syndrome research center, said that more than 60% of her patients with the syndrome meet the case definition of FM as well, which reflects at least in part the fact that the FM definition is looser and more inclusive while the chronic fatigue syndrome definition has many exclusionary criteria.

Dr. Bradley added that a number of recent studies have also shown a familial aggregation of pain sensitivity. The studies show that first-degree relatives of patients with FM tend to have the "same sorts of unusual sensitivities to pain and abnormal pain responses," even though this isn't always manifested as FM.

Alternative Health Care Can Be Valuable in the Treatment of Fibromyalgia

John R. Bomar

In the following viewpoint John R. Bomar explains the belief of some practitioners of alternative medicine that systemic toxicity resulting from poor diet is a cause of fibromyalgia. In his opinion, people should be primarily vegetarians. He also believes that few patients consume enough water. In addition, Bomar claims that chiropractic spinal manipulation is often beneficial, but because fibromyalgia patients have heightened sensitivity to pain, it must be done very carefully and should be preceded by massage. Less controversially, he states that moderate exercise is essential to recovery from fibromyalgia and that attitude affects health. Bomar is a chiropractor who practices in Arkansas.

They usually come in "hurting all over." They often are depressed, discouraged and not sleeping well. They frequently arise stiff and sore in the morning, feeling fatigued. They have suffered bouts of irritable

SOURCE: John R. Bomar, "Fibromyalgia Patients: A Real Pain in the Muscles and Fibers," *Dynamic Chiropractic*, June 3, 2008, pp. 31, 35. Copyright © 2008 MPA Media. Reproduced by permission.

bowel symptoms. They appear anxious and feel chronically "burned out." According to the American Academy of Rheumatology (ACR), 3 million to 6 million Americans suffer from some form of the disorder fibromyalgia. A majority of them are women of childbearing age. However, fibromyalgia also can affect children, the elderly and men.

Conventional Wisdom

Fibromyalgia is characterized by widespread muscle, ligament and tendon pain, chronic fatigue and multiple areas of trigger-point tenderness. The condition was recognized in previous generations, but was known by other names such as muscular rheumatism, fibrocitis and tension myalgia.

Allopathic [standard] medicine does not recognize a cause for fibromyalgia. Current thinking centers on internal imbalances that cause an increase in sensitivity to pain signals. Sleep disturbance, past injury, infection, metabolic muscle changes, hormonal imbalance and stress are other considerations in the etiology of fibromyalgia. Interestingly for chiropractors, abnormalities of sympathetic nervous system function also have been postulated as a factor in its etiology.

Diagnosing fibromyalgia can be difficult, as it can mimic many other disorders. The ACR has established the criteria of at least three months of chronic widespread pain and tenderness in at least 11 of 18 specific trigger-point sites.

Medical treatment involves recommendations for aerobic exercise such as swimming and walking, heat and massage treatments, antidepressant and analgesic/muscle relaxant medications, sleep aids, physical therapy and relaxation techniques of guided imagery. Many physicians also recommend stress-management strategies, improved diet and a healthier lifestyle.

The Alternative and Holistic Perspective

Many in the alternative health care community see systemic toxicity as a fundamental consideration in fibromyalgia. They believe physiological disturbances from impaired heart, liver, lung and kidney function are at the root of the problem. As we know, the liver and kidneys are the primary detoxifiers of the body. Thus, systemic toxicity (autointoxication) can be the end result of impaired function in these organs.

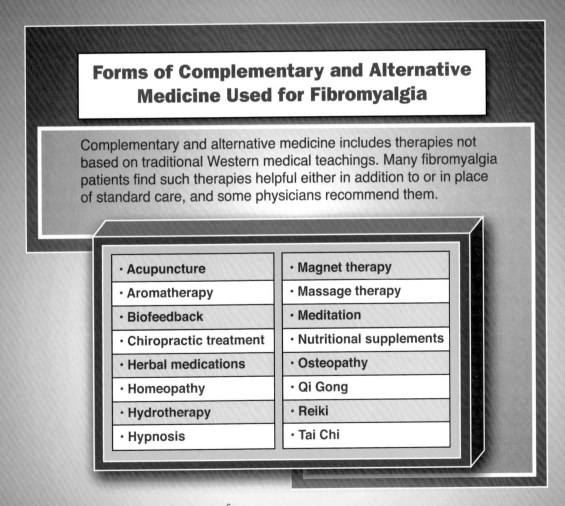

Forms of Complementary and Alternative Medicine Used for Fibromyalgia

Complementary and alternative medicine includes therapies not based on traditional Western medical teachings. Many fibromyalgia patients find such therapies helpful either in addition to or in place of standard care, and some physicians recommend them.

• Acupuncture	• Magnet therapy
• Aromatherapy	• Massage therapy
• Biofeedback	• Meditation
• Chiropractic treatment	• Nutritional supplements
• Herbal medications	• Osteopathy
• Homeopathy	• Qi Gong
• Hydrotherapy	• Reiki
• Hypnosis	• Tai Chi

[Compiled by the editor.]

As specialists in neuromusculoskeletal disorders, we can forget that life itself, as we know it, is basically an electromagnetic phenomenon. In the East, they describe this essential internal energy reserve as *qi*. Some even see the liver and kidneys as akin to batteries of the body, with the liver serving as the positive pole and the kidneys as the negative. When these organs are deficient in functioning, the body's "battery" is said to be run down. Chronic fatigue, low vitality and organic depression are the result, features common in fibromyalgia patients.

Just as the internal composition of a regular battery can influence its charge, the inner atmosphere of the human body can influence its vitality and strength. Scientific evidence increasingly points to the fact that, for maximum health and wellness, we should be primarily vegetarians, with fruits and vegetables making up the great majority (70 percent to 80 percent) of consumed food. Good-quality grains, nuts and oils, dairy and lean meats should make up the other 20 percent to 30 percent. This has an anti-inflammatory effect and creates an alkalized internal atmosphere, which also produces the health benefit of discouraging reproduction of most pH-dependent human pathogens that are acid-loving.

A Therapeutic Regimen

Systemic toxicity demands that primary attention be given to the basic processes of adequate hydration and increased eliminations. My personal observation is that very few patients consume sufficient water for bodily needs, which is estimated to be at least 64 ounces (eight glasses) daily. They tend to try and substitute colas, teas and coffee, all of which are diuretic, resulting in little or no net fluid gain. Almost all human biochemical processes require hydrogen. Without sufficient hydration, these processes slow, contributing to fatigue and accentuating the accumulation of metabolic wastes. Under- or frank [clinically evident]

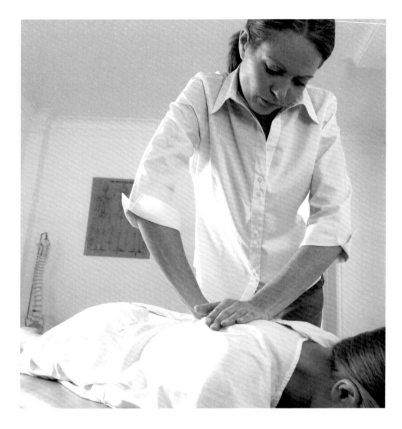

Manual therapy in the form of spinal adjustment and massage has proven beneficial to many fibromyalgia patients. **(Adam Gault/ Photo Researchers, Inc.)**

dehydration also slows bowel motility, which contributes to reabsorption of toxic waste into the general circulation. "Water is medicine" is my advice to these patients, along with a cleansing diet of fresh fruits and vegetables. Enemas and laxatives also might be useful in internal cleansing, especially if a patient has been constipated. For the most severe cases of long-standing autointoxication, I recommend patients consider a series of colonic irrigations.

Manual therapy (spinal adjustment and massage) will prove very beneficial to most sufferers of fibromyalgia. Spinal biomechanical lesions and nerve "impingements" almost always reflexly stimulate some degree of associated regional muscular spasm, which leads to a relative ischemia and toxemia in and around the tissue. Chronic, longstanding myospasm creates adhesions, scarring and fibrosis.

In applying any form of manual therapy to those with fibromyalgia, one should take great care in the early stages. Since these patients have heightened sensitization to pain, overly aggressive, ham-fisted approaches to treatment often will backfire, creating such additional suffering pain as to lose a patient. In the early days, many osteopaths and chiropractors recommended sustained anti-inflammatory measures such as repetitive cold packs and a series of hands-on massages before even attempting spinal manipulation for those with severe pain syndromes.

In recommending dietary changes to patients, I have found it beneficial to discuss the "opportunity of illness." While this sounds counterintuitive, I explain that the reason for the pain signal is to alert them to the underlying condition that needs to be changed for the better. I believe most frank pathology is the result of long-term imbalance in normal physiology, often caused by errors in diet and lifestyle and exacerbated by past injury or chronic inflammation.

Some form of moderate exercise such as walking or swimming is essential to recovery from fibromyalgia. Also frequently beneficial is the discipline of yoga-type stretching. Being out in the open as much as possible while exercising has been shown to be superior to time spent inside on the treadmill. Both walking and swimming mobilize needed lymphatic flow in the body. Arm swings pump this "dirty seawater" back into the veins under the clavicle, where it eventually is cleansed. Of course, the skin and lungs play an important role in metabolic waste elimination as well, so heating a well-hydrated body (hot baths, sauna) to create increased heart rate, perspiration and aerobic breathing also is beneficial.

Finally, "the mind is the builder, or the mind is the slayer" is a well-recognized axiom that acknowledges the

FAST FACT

Not all doctors are willing to take fibromyalgia patients. Some do not believe the disease exists, and many more do not know how to treat it. Also, because most people with fibromyalgia have many different symptoms, treating them is complex and time-consuming.

health or disease effect of attitude and emotion. Fear-filled, angry folk who habitually engage in what motivational speaker Zig Ziglar called "stinking thinking," eventually pay a price in their body's lack of wellness. Taking in lots of information that creates distress and inner turmoil, while feeling completely helpless to improve the situation, is what Hans Selye (who coined the term *stress*) called "pathologically alarming" to us human animals. Conversely, time spent in reading and positive thought of our highest purposes and ideals can contribute substantially to the healing process.

Fibromyalgia can be healed and left behind in a person's life experience. Recognizing its multi-faceted causes and taking a comprehensive approach to its treatment is essential to success in your efforts as true healer.

Patients Must Fight Health Insurers to Get Fibromyalgia Medication

Steve Twedt

In the following article Steve Twedt explains that although new drugs have recently been approved for treating fibromyalgia, insurance companies often do not cover them because they do not consider them medically necessary. Many patients are having trouble getting them, Twedt reports, and doctors find this frustrating. They feel it is wrong for insurers to let financial considerations override medical decisions, he says. Twedt is an award-winning journalist for the *Pittsburgh Post-Gazette* who has written extensively about patient safety issues.

With the Food and Drug Administration's [FDA's] approval of a second fibromyalgia medication last month [June 2008], you'd think the nation's estimated 10 million acute pain fibromyalgia sufferers would be delighted. Not quite.

SOURCE: Steve Twedt, "Fibromyalgia Patients Fight Insurers over Medication Coverage," *Pittsburgh Post-Gazette*, July 13, 2008. Copyright © 2008 PG Publishing Co., Inc. All rights reserved. Reproduced by permission.

While welcoming any new treatment, patients also know that insurance companies have been slow to cover Lyrica, which won FDA approval a year ago, and probably will have similar reluctance with Cymbalta, an antidepressant now approved for treating fibromyalgia. "There have been some insurers who take the stand that if they make it more and more difficult for patients to get these medications, they will go away," said Lynne Matallana, president and founder of the nonprofit National Fibromyalgia Association.

Insurance companies often do not consider Lyrica and Cymbalta medically necessary, and instead will stress lifestyle changes and steer patients to off-label pain relievers or alternative treatments such as relaxation techniques, physical therapy and biofeedback. "What they mean is 'fiscally necessary,'" said Dr. Leslie Tar, a local physician/attorney specializing in rheumatology who treats hundreds of fibromyalgia patients in the region. "They are using a financial definition for a medical problem."

When Ms. Matallana's Fibromyalgia Association sent e-mails two months ago asking members if they'd had trouble getting medication or finding a knowledgeable physician to help them, 800 people responded affirmatively the first weekend. "If you're really ill, it takes a lot of energy [to fill out a survey]. To have 800 people take the time to respond is quite extraordinary. We're going to have to come up with a way to convince third party payers that by getting a diagnosis and getting treatment, we are actually reducing costs," said Ms. Matallana.

Doctors Have Often Disagreed with Insurers

This is not the first time doctors and their patients have disagreed with insurers about what medications or procedures should be covered. But this latest example illustrates growing tensions in the struggle between containing health-care costs and helping ill people feel better.

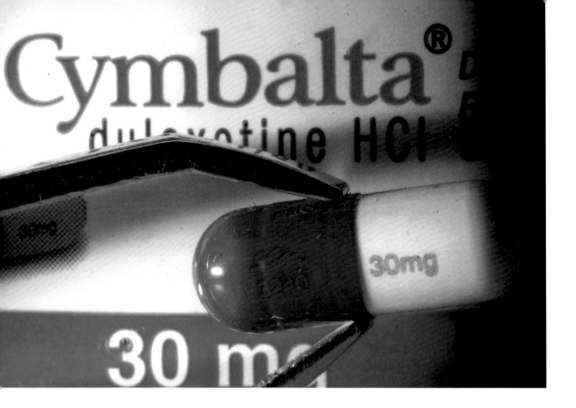

Many insurers do not consider drugs such as Cymbalta medically necessary to treat fibromyalgia, and many patients are financially unable to purchase the drugs on their own. (JB Reed/Landov)

Last year, Dr. Tar diagnosed Christine King, 57, of Carrick [Pennsylvania] with fibromyalgia after she had suffered severe pain for two years. A doctor she had seen previously had attributed her pain to arthritis. "I had a lot of muscle pain and stiffness, and I couldn't turn my head. It was just a constant pain," she said.

Dr. Tar prescribed both Lyrica and Cymbalta, as the medications work on different receptors in the brain. Ms. King went to her pharmacy, expecting to get the scripts filled for a $3 co-payment. "The pharmacist said the medication wasn't covered," she recalled. Her actual bill was close to $200.

With Dr. Tar's assistance, she successfully appealed the insurer's decision before an administrative law judge. She says she started feeling better within days of taking the medications, though she eventually stopped taking Lyrica because it made her sleepy. Today, she says her pain is less than half what it was. "Illness is a fight in itself, and having to fight for medication just makes it tougher."

Access to Lyrica is not a life-or-death proposition—and not all patients say they feel better after using it. But it's not a budget buster for insurance companies either.

Both Lyrica and Cymbalta treat fibromyalgia's main symptoms, an often-debilitating sensitivity to pain, rather than cure the disease. Diagnosis is made through an extensive physical exam; fibromyalgia cannot be detected by an X-ray or a blood test.

Fibromyalgia's amorphous nature—a *New York Times* story earlier this year raised the question of whether it is an actual disease—and the highly individualized effectiveness of the medications no doubt play into the calculus of deciding not to cover even FDA-approved medications.

But that misses the point, Dr. Tar said. "When I prescribe a medication and the insurance company says, 'no,' what am I supposed to do? I'm frustrated, and the patient is frustrated. They are limiting access to necessary medicine."

More than Half of Fibromyalgia Patients Lack Access to Medication

He estimates that about 30 percent to 40 percent of his fibromyalgia patients have health insurance that covers the medications. The others are directed to the "therapeutic alternatives." "And, what do you know? Those therapeutic alternatives are generics and are very cheap," Dr. Tar said. "This is a condition that has a treatment, but the patients lack access to it because of financial concerns. For the first time in my life, I'm finding this is happening more and more."

The FDA approves a medication only after it has been thoroughly tested and shown to be both safe and effective for treating a specific condition. Although FDA approval may make insurers more likely to

> **FAST FACT**
>
> Although there is still some controversy about whether fibromyalgia is a real disease, it has its own code for insurance forms. As Mark Pellegrino, the author of fifteen books on fibromyalgia, told the *New York Times*, "Insurance companies don't have a code number for a disease unless it's real."

Average Annual Cost of Fibromyalgia per Patient

Data is based on a 2009 study of 203 patients.

Physician office visits	$1,528
Diagnostic tests	$435
Prescription medications	$3,419
Emergency room visits	$43
Treatments	$1,798
Home health care services	$750
Total direct cost	**$7,973**
Indirect cost related to absenteeism	$1,228
Cost of disability payments and opportunity cost of not working	$9,470
Total indirect cost	**$10,698**

Taken from: Don L. Goldenberg et al., "What Is the True Cost of Fibromyalgia to Our Society: Results from a Cross-sectional Survey in the United States," ACR/ARHP Annual Scientific Meeting, October 18, 2009. http://aacr.conex.com/acr/2009/webprogram/Paper16264.html.

cover a medication, FDA has no authority to make them cover it.

Policies differ from insurer to insurer. [Pennsylvania-based insurer] Highmark administers many different policies, so some employers cover the medications and others don't.

The UPMC [University of Pittsburgh Medical Center] Health Plan covers Lyrica, but requires prior authorization in which the physician must document the condition and previous attempts to treat it. The plan is still reviewing whether it will cover Cymbalta.

Coventry Healthcare, parent company for Health-America, also covers both medications, according to a company spokesman, adding that FDA approval does not "necessarily move the drug to a first line recommendation."

But not all preauthorization protocols are created equal, said Dr. Tar. "I fight with [HealthAmerica] continually as a patient advocate, and they are the least liberal in allowing for Lyrica."

While preauthorization is better than flat-out denial, Dr. Tar said it could have a similar effect if the process is too onerous. "Doctors are so busy, they are not interested in jumping through additional hoops. So they are being taught by the insurance companies to take the path of least resistance. And that's exactly what the insurance companies want. It's about the money. It's a way to decrease costs by undermining access to medication."

People with Fibromyalgia Are Not Protected by the Americans with Disabilities Act

Mitzi Baker

The following article by Mitzi Baker discusses the difficulty fibromyalgia patients have in getting accommodations made for their disability at work. According to Baker, individuals with "invisible" disabilities have to prove that they are sick, and because they are often stigmatized, some do not disclose their illness. Of those who do, she asserts, some have supportive employers, but many have to seek protection under the Americans with Disabilities Act (ADA). This is difficult for them to obtain because the Supreme Court has interpreted the ADA in a way that allows a quick judgment to be made without a jury. In most cases legal action to prevent such judgments has been unsuccessful. Therefore, Baker reports, Congress has proposed modifying the ADA to restore its original intent of protecting everyone who is disabled. Baker is a science and medical writer at Stanford University School of Medicine.

SOURCE: Mitzi Baker, "Elusive but Attainable: Justice for Workers Afflicted with Fibromyalgia," *Journal of Workplace Rights*, vol. 13, April 2008, pp. 201–206, 208–10, 212–14. © 2008, Baywood Publishing Co., Inc. Reproduced by permission.

Individuals who suffer from controversial diagnoses of ailments with uncertain causes that are virtually impossible for casual observers to detect are considered to be people with "invisible" disabilities. These individuals, who often suffer from conditions such as chronic pain syndrome, posttraumatic stress disorder, chronic fatigue syndrome, or severe fibromyalgia, may appear "normal" to people with whom they interact casually, but they may be disabled. Because they appear "normal," people with invisible disabilities are often placed in the awkward position of having to rebut the presumption of "normalcy."

The distinction between visible and invisible disability is not always obvious. One analysis suggests that invisible disabilities may meet all or any of the following conditions: (1) they may involve a disabling condition that cannot be easily ascertained by someone who is merely looking at the disabled person; (2) the individuals concerned may be at heightened risk for the recurrence of episodes that are painful, life-threatening, or activity-limiting; (3) individuals in this category severely limit the duration of their interactions in everyday social situations; and (4) their diagnoses may involve interpretation and require the use of judgment. Consequently, an individual with an invisible disability must point out the existence of his or her disability to others. This is no easy task, considering that many individuals with invisible disabilities are stigmatized and are subject to some form of rejection, humiliation, or social disapproval in today's society. Generally, what one cannot see with the naked eye will require further confirmation or proof; thus, individuals with invisible disabilities are faced with a serious challenge. To be able-bodied in today's social and economic spheres is a privilege; those that fail to conform to the able-bodied standard are considered socially invisible and continue to be stigmatized and disadvantaged. This stigma constitutes a major obstacle for these individuals and presents them with a dilemma: whether they should disclose a disability or not.

Should Persons with Invisible Disabilities Disclose Them?

Persons with invisible disabilities must inevitably provide sufficient evidence of their disabilities, often in the form of expert medical evidence. Employers have long considered such evidence as authoritative and credible. Unfortunately, however, in most cases, for individuals with invisible disabilities who suffer from chronic pain, depression, or severe anxiety there are no well-defined or objective tests that can readily identify their disabling conditions. Thus, the general consensus has been that several doctors need to confirm that an invisible disability, in fact, exists, before an individual will be considered disabled. This is partly due to current societal assumptions that these individuals may be "cheaters" or "malingerers" who are trying to obtain special treatment at the expense of others.

The challenge of providing convincing proof can be overwhelming and may cause some persons to refrain from disclosing their disability to others. Additionally, teaching others about their condition carries the risk of such consequences as isolation, indifference, and disbelief, a refusal to accommodate what the other person cannot see as a disability, or the disclosure of excessive personal information once the Pandora's box of disclosure is open.

On the other hand, silence may pose an even greater threat to the well-being of disabled individuals, exacerbating their disabilities and deepening their invisibility [J.E.] Beatty and [S.L.] Kirby identified this challenge when they wrote that "invisibility creates a dilemma for employees seeking the benefits of legal protection against discrimination in the workplace because to receive the benefits they must first disclose their situation. . . . Yet, the act of disclosing their difference is potentially career limiting because in doing so they create the grounds for possible stigma and discrimination." . . .

Legal Support in Lieu of Employer Support

Persons with invisible disabilities can benefit from destigmatization and can create a more nurturing work environment by obtaining moral and professional support from their supervisors and managers. Managerial awareness and support go a long way to improve the overall employer-employee relationship. However, when a breakdown in this relationship has occurred, most often the affected employees seek the legal protections accorded them through the Americans with Disabilities Act (ADA).

The ADA generally protects against practices that discriminate on the basis of a qualifying disability when the employee would be able to perform satisfactory work with a "reasonable accommodation." In order to qualify for protection, an individual with an invisible disability must prove the existence of a disability as defined by the ADA. Congress understood that adverse actions based upon a

President George H.W. Bush signs the Americans With Disabilities Act into law on July 26, 1990. (AP Images)

person's physical or mental impairment are often unrelated to the limitation caused by the impairment itself. Instead of following congressional expectations that the term "disability" would be interpreted broadly in the ADA, decisions and opinions by the Supreme Court have unduly narrowed the broad scope of protection afforded by the ADA, thereby eliminating protection for a broad range of individuals whom Congress intended to protect.

The Supreme Court and lower courts have interpreted the act with broad latitude, resulting in conflicting and unpredictable outcomes for individuals with an invisible disability. In the majority of cases, these individuals face an uphill battle, mainly because most employers file a motion for summary judgment, which allows the speedy disposition of a conflict without benefit of trial. Most employers are aware of the lack of traditional clinical evidence such as laboratory tests and X-rays, which are commonly used to prove the existence and extent of a medical condition and thus to prove the existence of a disability. Courts insist that plaintiffs overcome this first obstacle before the courts will examine the merits of any adverse actions. . . .

Who Is Disabled and What Are Reasonable Accommodations?

The ADA defines a "disabled individual" as one who
- has a physical or mental impairment that substantially limits one or more of the person's major life activities;
- has a record of such an impairment; or
- is regarded as having such an impairment.

First, a plaintiff must show that she suffers from a physical or mental impairment. Second, the plaintiff must identify the activity claimed as being impaired and establish that it constitutes a "major life activity." Third, the plaintiff must show that her impairment "substantially

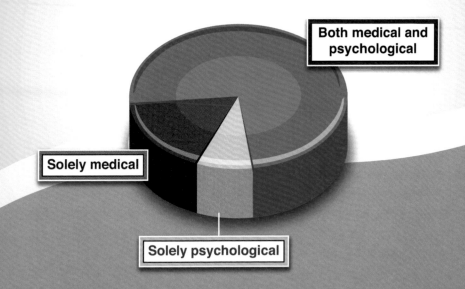

How Doctors View Fibromyalgia

In one survey, approximately 75 percent of doctors said fibromyalgia is both a medical and a psychological condition; less than 20 percent said it is solely a medical condition; and less than 10 percent said it is solely a psychological condition.

Both medical and psychological

Solely medical

Solely psychological

Taken from: *Internal Medicine News*, "Fibromyalgia Care Varies Among Specialties," January 1, 2009.

limits" a major life activity. The Supreme Court has clarified that the identified major life activity must be "of central importance to daily life." ...

A qualified individual with a disability is a person who meets the legitimate skill, experience, education, or other requirements of an employment position that she or he holds or seeks, and who can perform the "essential functions" (i.e., the fundamental job duties) of the position with or without reasonable accommodation.

The Equal Employment Opportunities Commission defines reasonable accommodation as a modification or adjustment to a job, the work environment, or the way things are usually done that enables a qualified individual with a disability to enjoy an equal employment opportunity. Reasonable accommodations generally fall within three categories: (1) changes in the job application process in order to enable a qualified applicant to be considered for a job; (2) changes in the work environment or the manner in which the job is performed; (3) changes in order to enable an employee with a disability to enjoy benefits and privileges of employment that are equal to those of others. . . .

The Job Accommodation Network gives us some potentially useful workplace scenarios pertinent to individuals with chronic pain and fibromyalgia:

- An appointments secretary was reprimanded for poor attendance due to chronic pain. She was provided with periodic rest breaks when at work and allowed to telecommute part-time.
- A human resource manager suffered from chronic pain due to a car accident. He was having difficulty getting to work on time. He was accommodated with a flexible schedule to allow him more time to access public transit.
- A switchboard operator with chronic pain and fibromyalgia was accommodated with flexible scheduling, rest breaks, and an adjustable workstation. The adjustable workstation allowed her to alternate between a sitting and a standing position.
- An individual with chronic pain due to a back injury was having difficulty sitting throughout the day. She was accommodated with a reclining workstation.
- A medical technician with chronic pain was restricted with regard to doing repetitive work that involved typing throughout the day. He was transferred to another job requiring less repetition.
- An assembly line worker with chronic pain was having difficulty standing for long periods. He was ac-

commodated with a sit-lean stool and antifatigue matting. . . .

Fibromyalgia and ADA Litigation

In "New diagnoses and the ADA: A case study of fibromyalgia and multiple chemical sensitivity," Ruby Afram studied fibromyalgia and ADA litigation and made the following observations:

- Motions for summary judgment by the defendants in ADA claims with regard to fibromyalgia were granted or affirmed in 33 of the 37 cases studied (almost 90%); a motion to dismiss for failure to state a claim was granted in another case.
- In only four cases did the plaintiffs survive summary judgment.
- In none of the cases is there a record of the plaintiff prevailing at trial. It is possible that these cases were settled out of court in a manner favorable to the plaintiff or are still in litigation.
- Based upon published opinions, fibromyalgia cases under the ADA appear to reflect an almost total lack of success for the plaintiffs.
- Analysis suggests a greater focus on the nature of the disease in these cases.
- The cases in which courts have excluded evidence about fibromyalgia have been cases in which causation was the key to determining liability, and there still exists a relative consensus in the medical community that there is no known cause for fibromyalgia.
- The determination of whether an individual has a disability is not necessarily based on the name or diagnosis of the person's impairment, but rather on the effect that impairment has on the life of the individual. . . .

While most courts agree that fibromyalgia is a disability within the meaning of the ADA, the vast majority look to two important threshold issues: (1) whether an individual with fibromyalgia is substantially limited in a major life activity, and (2) whether the individual with fibromyalgia is a qualified individual with a disability as defined by the ADA. If the plaintiff meets these two criteria, the courts then concentrate on the following:

- whether the plaintiff's medical record is specific and detailed enough to include regular medical treatment documented on an ongoing basis;
- the severity, duration, and expected long-term impact on the individual's specific impairments; and
- whether (bearing in mind the fact that fibromyalgia has been a subjectively determined syndrome) the testimony of the plaintiff on the effects on his/her daily life is supported or at least not contradicted by the medical expert.

If the plaintiff can meet the above criteria, the judge or jury can infer that the individual has a disability under the ADA. . . .

Changes to ADA May Provide Truly Equal Protection

The cases that prevailed met the standards described above with credible medical evidence, supported by testimony by medical professionals, establishing a record of long-term care and establishing that the employers knew about the disability and did not accommodate the plaintiff's fibromyalgia. Moreover, the key factor was not the argument that fibromyalgia was not disabling in any respect (most courts agree that it is) but rather the question of how it affects daily life, whether it is substantial in manner, duration, and severity, and whether it has long-term consequences. The cases that failed did not establish the aforementioned facts and thus were denied ADA protection. Further, as noted above, fibromyalgia affects individuals in different ways, and the courts require genuine proof as to how it affects an individual and whether it meets the criteria to prove that its effects fall within the meaning of the ADA. . . .

Should drastic changes to the text of the ADA be proposed in order to resolve the problem of equal protection for individuals with serious medical conditions such as fibromyalgia? The answer to this inquiry is a resounding yes. . . .

Congress has noted that 90% of ADA plaintiffs lose their claims in court, and that many people with serious medical conditions are found not to be covered by the act. In response to the Supreme Court's decisions and opinions narrowing the scope of the statute, and in order to reinstate the original congressional intent regarding the definition of disability, Congress has proposed to clarify those sections of the act that should afford protection to all individuals with visible and invisible disabilities in two new bills, which I believe will be effective in achieving uniformity in answering the question, "What is a disability?" . . .

These modifications . . . would unquestionably create a brighter picture for individuals with invisible disabilities such as fibromyalgia and would allow them to obtain justice.

FAST FACT

According to the Fibromyalgia Network, studies show that approximately 25 percent of fibromyalgia patients receive some form of disability compensation at any given time.

CHAPTER 3

Personal Narratives About Fibromyalgia

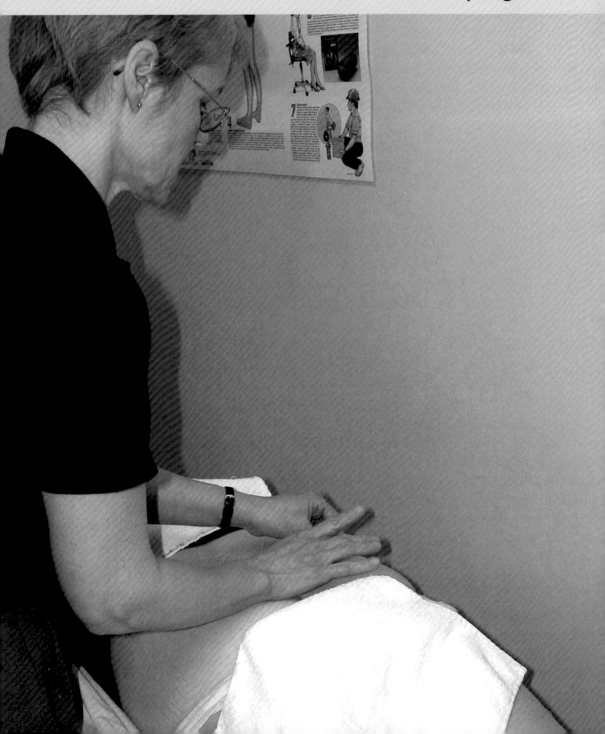

Living with Fibromyalgia in High School

Jerry Sauve

In the following article Jerry Sauve tells about growing up with fibromyalgia, which first struck him when he was about eight years old. He was sick so often in the fourth grade that his parents homeschooled him for a year, but when he returned to school he again had long absences and could not keep up with his homework. In high school he was determined not to miss school, but he found this was not realistic, as he could not fall asleep at night and so was unable to stay awake during the day. Finally, he dropped out of school, and his health began to improve, Sauve reveals. When he got better sleep, his pain became more manageable. Eventually he got a high school diploma through homeschooling and was able to enjoy life with his friends. He still had bad days, Sauve reports, but he also had many good ones. As of 2008 Sauve was attending college and was planning to become a high school teacher.

SOURCE: Jerry Sauve, *Fibromyalgia: The Complete Guide from Medical Experts and Patients*, Sharon Ostalecki, ed. Copyright © 2008 by Jones and Bartlett Publishers, Sudbury, MA. www.jbpub.com. All rights reserved. Reproduced by permission.

Photo on facing page. Some fibromyalgia patients opt for weekly acupuncture treatments. (© John T. Fowler/Alamy)

My name is Jerry Sauve. I am 18 years old and pass my days either working part-time at the Detroit Zoo or spending time with my girlfriend and her family. I also try to get out at least once or twice a week to play two grueling hours of hockey with friends. I'm an all-around athletic guy, known in most of my circles for being the comedian . . . or the kid who won $1,000 and a brand new Corvette. But that's another story. (All right, all right, I only won the car for a week, but at least I've got your attention.)

In a little more than a month I start my freshman year of college. I plan to teach at the high school where I spent my freshman and sophomore years barely keeping my head above water.

Oh yeah, there's one other thing—I have fibromyalgia. . . .

It started when I was about 8 years old, and it lasted (at full force) until about two years ago. It stopped rather suddenly. (Or, at least I feel close enough to "normal" that I would hardly know the difference.)

From birth to around age 8, I was a reasonably healthy child. You could probably say I was a bit sensitive, even as young children go. I started second grade in a new school, a much smaller school, when I first started getting sick. At first, it just seemed like I was a natural magnet for whatever flu was going around. I constantly had the flu, a cold, an ear infection, a sinus infection, stomach problems, or I just didn't feel good for one reason or another. All the same stuff other kids have, but with little time in between. Nonetheless, I still did well in school. . . .

After fourth grade, my absences became enough of a problem that my parents considered home-schooling me. It seemed that I was much better in the afternoon than in the morning. Home-schooling would let me sleep an extra hour or two without missing classroom instruction and having to make up the homework. . . .

By the end of home-schooling for the fifth grade, having had almost nothing educational happen, my parents decided I should go back to public school. We thought that maybe a year off had built up my immune system and had made me stronger. I'd recently learned how to ride a bike and had been out riding daily. This combination of exercise, fresh air, and plenty of sleep was a big step in the right direction.

I probably was the strongest I'd been in my life. Though I was keenly aware of how much school I had missed, I still didn't really consider myself sick—just unlucky, I'd gotten so used to my condition that I really hadn't thought much about all the time in doctors' offices and hospitals, except that it was no fun and that I was glad to be done with it. I felt pretty confident that I was. . . .

Because of the difficulty of maintaining a normal schedule, some students suffering from fibromyalgia are schooled at home. (© **Stock Connection Blue/Alamy**)

Missing School Too Often

Unfortunately, I bet it wasn't a month before I started getting sick again, missing several days or a week at a time. Before long, a week at a time became two weeks, two weeks became three, and by seventh grade, weeks became months. Yes, months.

I struggled. I was torn; physically and mentally, I was overwhelmed. Although I was still relatively healthy, I struggled under the load of excessive homework. Now I had three to five hours a night on top of being sick.

I fell so far behind that by the time I started something, the rest of the class was finishing it. Whether I went to school hardly mattered, because it was virtually impossible for me to catch up, much less participate. In addition to this pressure, other factors began to weigh in.

First, I couldn't just be one of "them" anymore. If it's been a while since your school days, I remind you how important it is to *not* be different. Even if you don't fit in, you can get by, so long as you don't stand out. And nothing makes you stand out more than being gone for a month or more at a time—while everyone thinks you died or are in the hospital—and then returning out of the blue.

Fortunately, when I was actually at school, I was both "the sick kid" and "the really funny kid." I knew that if I could ever stop being sick, I could be "the really funny kid who used to be sick all of the time," which was a definite and glorious upgrade, if indeed it was in reach.

Unfortunately, it simply wasn't. By eighth grade, I'd missed almost all but the first two or three months and the final two weeks of the year. There were kids who had actually forgotten about me, that I had to reintroduce myself to. These were kids I'd gone to school with for two years already! Ouch indeed.

The usual response when I was remembered, was "Oh man, I heard you'd died." I am serious. And after awhile, I would hardly blink. It became the expected, the assumed.

Worse yet was that I didn't have a label for what was wrong with me and why I was never there. I didn't have a name for the disease I struggled against, something that people could understand. I know that a lot of people, young and old, probably didn't even believe I was sick.

Between the hours of homework I could never keep up with and being sick, I spent all my time indoors alone, wondering why I was sick all the time and whether I'd ever have a normal life. I went out of my way to avoid spending time with other people, because I'd closed myself off to the rest of the world in frustration, depression, and self-loathing. Then there were all the doctors' appointments, spending three hours in waiting rooms. Eventually I gave up on Western medicine altogether, though I appreciate the few doctors who legitimately tried and cared and were frustrated in their efforts to discover what direction to take treatment, in what form, against what condition, and so on.

Starting my sophomore year, I was determined not to miss school, no matter how hard it was, no matter how sick I was. But that goal just wasn't realistic. I still couldn't fall asleep at night and would only *begin* getting drowsy by morning. Therefore, it was nearly impossible for me to stay awake until the end of the day, much less pay attention and retain anything. The muscle aches and the joint pain were worst in the morning, and lack of sleep made them worse. I had stomach problems as well. . . .

So, there I was starting my sophomore year, trying to get through a full week of school on little or no sleep, exhausted, with muscle aches and joint pain thrown in to take care of any dull moments. This was simply not a realistic routine for me, and again I found myself way over my head and well past my limit. I finally decided I'd had enough.

Dropping Out

I had a long talk with my mother in which I pleaded my case, and she agreed to take me out of school. I needed to be able to sleep whenever I could and to get as much rest as I needed. I also needed to cut down on the incredible amount of stress and pressure of homework and grades. I needed to take care of myself, get control of my life, and take it from there. I was too sick too often, and I had zero quality of life. . . .

So, I dropped out of school and proceeded to wait all night to be able to fall asleep around 9 or 10 in the morning, and then sleep all day. This is not as much fun as it sounds. Believe me, when your parent(s) have to get up for work in the morning, you are severely limited in what you can do on a schedule that has you awake all night and asleep all day. . . .

But things soon got better. A great weight was lifted from my shoulders (not to mention my body) when I was freed of all the stress of the homework, of the bad grades, of always being behind, and of never doing anything good enough for anyone. With all that gone, I started sleeping. . . .

I was falling asleep 10–15 minutes earlier every night, and soon I was falling asleep earlier than I ever had! At eight o'clock in the evening I was going to bed; at six o'clock in the morning I was waking up feeling like a million bucks. And the better sleep I got, the more manageable the pain was in my muscles and joints. The more manageable the pain got, the more I was up to doing during the day, and the better I felt inside and out. In other words, sleeping well made all the difference in the world. And that was just the beginning.

The more I took care of myself and learned to listen to my body (you have my word that "listening to your body" is more than an obnoxious, beaten-to-death medical cliché), the better things got. Suddenly, I wasn't feeling bad at all. And I could start taking steps towards getting my life back together.

I started home-schooling again, now old enough and close enough to the finish line that I could motivate myself to teach myself, through a wonderful program called the American School.

Managing Fibromyalgia Intuitively

Amazingly, just a year later, here I am: 18 years old, with a girlfriend of two years, attending college, playing hockey with my friends, going to bed every night and waking up every morning, holding down a good job, and genuinely enjoying life. Life is so good that sometimes, I wonder if fibromyalgia's still in my system anymore. And then, every once in awhile, I'll wake up with a very clear reminder that it is. And at certain points of the day, I still feel it, some days worse than others, depending on where I've been and what I've done; but this is *nothing* compared to being unable to function and enjoy life. After all, everyone has limitations.

So what's the secret? What's my advice for someone my age or younger who's struggling with school, with life, or in any way with fibromyalgia?

Look, there is no secret. It's common sense:

- First, know that whatever you have to do, you're going to survive.
- Take care of *yourself* first, and let the rest fall into place. If you can't handle the life that you're trying to live, figure out what changes you need to make and make them. Think outside the box.
- If you have trouble sleeping like I did, discuss it with your parents, your physician, and anyone else who could help you.
- Finally, consider home-schooling if you're ready for it. . . .

Home-schooling isn't the answer for every young person with fibromyalgia. Yet everyone has parts of their daily life that fibromyalgia makes sensationally difficult, and the best advice I can give is to explore your options. Never forget that you *have* options. They are endless. Talk with your doctor, talk with your family.

You go to a doctor for help, but sometimes there's not a lot they can do, especially for something like fibromyalgia. Even when they can help you, you need to look for other things that you can do to help yourself. Everyone is different, every body is different, but some things are universally easy, and listening to your body is one of them.

On that note, figure out when it's OK to push yourself and when it's not. Part of listening to your body is learning your limits. . . .

I would also like to bring up a common grievance among fibromyalgia sufferers: that we are not always taken seriously, because we don't look as sick as we feel—if we look sick at all. Because of that some people don't believe that we are suffering. Although I might've argued with myself when life wasn't as easy, I know now that not looking as sick as you feel, and having some people not believe you, is *not* the hardest part of fibromyalgia. You are you and they are them. You must know what you know and understand that some people either don't want to or can't understand what you're going through.

Like any difficult situation, your attitude is the key. In this case, the glass can either be half empty or half full. Although some days I felt miserable and no one could tell, on a good day, I felt like a million bucks. . . .

Recognize that no matter how well you engineer your daily life to cooperate with your body, you are going to have bad days. I feel great and I still have bad days. That's what fibromyalgia is. The trick is to have more good days than bad days, and if you are, you're already winning. Beyond that, there's not much more you can do. There is no cleansing process. You have fibromyalgia, and chances are you always will. But, take it from me, someone who was completely hopeless and cynical, that fibromyalgia is manageable.

FAST FACT

When the National Fibromyalgia Association launched a campaign to get ten thousand "fans" on its Facebook page by October 1, 2009, to help raise awareness of fibromyalgia, it reached its goal well over a month ahead of the deadline.

Being Diagnosed with Fibromyalgia

Adrienne Dellwo

In the following article Adrienne Dellwo tells about her first attack of fibromyalgia, which occurred while she was at work and was so intense that she had to go to the emergency room. At first the paramedics thought she might be having a heart attack but soon found that her heart was normal. The doctor at the hospital could not tell what was wrong. She recovered but later had another attack of pain that took her to the emergency room again. This was followed by months of medical tests that showed nothing, Dellwo reports. Finally she went to a rheumatologist who diagnosed her as having fibromyalgia. She had to learn how to manage the condition, which meant giving up her job as a TV news producer in order to reduce stress. She hopes that someday a cure for fibromyalgia will be found. Dellwo is a journalist who has worked for both television and newspapers and has extensive experience researching and writing about health-related issues. She was diagnosed with fibromyalgia in 2006.

SOURCE: Adrienne Dellwo, "Thrown Off Course: Fibromyalgia Enters My Life," About.com, January 12, 2009. © 2009 Adrienne Dellwo. http://chronicfatigue.about.com/od/diagnosingfmscfs/a/off_ course.htm. Used with permission of About, Inc., which can be found online at www.about.com. All rights reserved.

The pain started while I was sitting at my desk. It wasn't pain at first—just a tightening. I noticed it distantly at first, vaguely thinking it was the start of one of the severe allergic reactions I'd been having all spring. I used my inhaler and washed down an antihistamine with the last of my latte.

A few minutes later it got painful. I now noticed the tightening was not in my throat, but in my chest.

I tried to dismiss it, but the pain grew more intense. My heart was soon pounding. I became short of breath and a bit dizzy. The pain started to radiate through to my back. I got online and searched for "heart attack symptoms" and found a check list: uncomfortable pressure in the center of the chest lasting more than a few minutes? Yep. Pain spreading to the shoulders, neck or arms? Yes, as a matter of fact. Lightheadedness, fainting, sweating, nausea or shortness of breath? Yes, no, a little, yes, and oh, yeah! Increased or irregular heart rate? Uh-huh. Feeling of impending doom? After reading this list, definitely!

I had to tell someone what was going on, but I was frightened and confused. I didn't want to say I was having a heart attack only to have it be nothing, but I also didn't want to drop dead on the floor or wait too long for treatment.

I shakily stood up and walked over to a small group of people. "Something's really wrong and I'm not sure what," I said. I then told them what symptoms I was having.

Everyone's first thought was that this was another allergic reaction—I'd been in the emergency room [ER] with two. The pain was so bad I could barely stand, so someone wheeled over a chair. Someone else offered to call my husband. "He's asleep," I gasped. "He won't hear the phone."

I scribbled down the name of my husband's 76-year-old grandmother, who lived close to us and was the only relative likely to be home. Someone called her while two others pushed me, still in the chair, down a little hallway to the back door. Another co-worker was pulling a car up to drive me to the ER.

A Trip to the Emergency Room

I tried to stand up but couldn't. I was hunched over in agony, barely able to breathe. "This isn't allergies," I coughed out. Someone called 9-1-1. Someone else brought me aspirin and water. Everyone in the company who was trained in CPR [cardiopulmonary resuscitation] suddenly appeared, as did my boss and his boss. That hallway was getting crowded!

Finally the paramedics arrived and got me into the ambulance. Believing I was having a heart attack, they started an IV [intravenous therapy], put nitrogen tablets under my tongue, asked if I'd taken aspirin, and hooked me up to a machine to check my heart. Then, one of the paramedics reacted in mild surprise. My heart was doing just fine, beating along at a normal, if slightly elevated, rhythm. They then asked more questions, checked more vitals, and decided they didn't know what was wrong.

Just as I was being wheeled in, a nurse asked if I was Mrs. Dellwo, because if so, my husband had called and was on his way. I knew I could count on Grandma!

By now, the pain was easing up a bit. It still ached, and I had intense spasms that made me ball up in pain, but it wasn't constant anymore.

When my husband, Joe, arrived, he looked almost as bad as I felt—pale, scared, exhausted. After working a graveyard shift, he'd only been asleep for about two hours when his grandma came knocking. I can only imagine how scared he was as he drove across town to the hospital.

The ER doctor had me shot up with pain killers, then ordered blood work, a chest x-ray, and an EKG [electrocardiogram]. We'd have to wait on the blood work of course, but the other tests showed nothing. Nothing at all. This was not cardiac, nor was it a broken or damaged rib.

They gave me what the nurse called a "G.I. cocktail," a mixture of drugs that numbed everything as I swallowed it. If it helped, this was a gastric problem. If it didn't, it wasn't. Well, it didn't.

The doctor [said] I probably had a soft-tissue injury where my top rib connected to my breast bone that was causing a lot of pain and inflammation. I didn't really buy it, but what else could it be?

By then I was feeling a little achy, but not horrible. Then, just as I was about to be sent home, the pain came back, and my husband witnessed exactly what had led to our being there. So I got more pain meds, and the doctor handed Joe a stack of prescriptions. They were for pain, nausea, acid reflux and inflammation. I thought, "That shows just how much they really don't know what's going on." I was ordered to follow up with my regular doctor immediately.

Months of Medical Tests

After a few days, it was clear this was no soft-tissue injury. My doctor couldn't find any solid leads, even after extensive testing. I missed several days of work and still didn't feel good when I went back.

Then one night Joe rushed me to the ER with pain down lower. If it hadn't been for a CT [computed tomography] scan showing my appendix was normal, a surgeon would have been going in after it. My regular doctor soon knew us by name and was calling me at home to check on things. I'd get a little better, then a little worse—sometimes a lot worse. Still, no one could find anything wrong. This went on for about five months.

Through our own diligent research, Joe and I had decided I most likely had an autoimmune disease, and Lupus

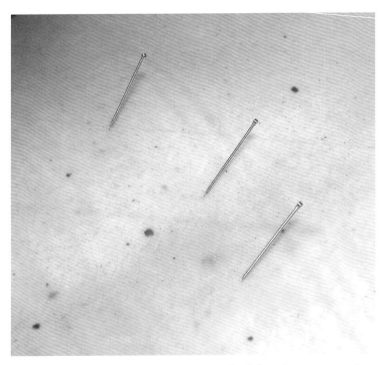

Acupuncture therapists apply needles to a patient's lower back to relieve the symptoms of fibromyalgia. (© John T. Fowler/Alamy)

seemed like a top candidate. We asked for the appropriate tests and got them—but again, found nothing.

A few weeks later, I sat in a rheumatologist's office and, after pretty extensive questioning, she started pushing on certain spots and asking if they hurt. They did, nearly every one. At long last we had a diagnosis. I had fibromyalgia.

That began the next phase, which was learning about the condition and managing it. That has involved stress reduction (I'm no longer a TV news producer), vitamins and supplements, Chinese herbs and acupuncture. I know I can't be cured—not now, and perhaps not ever—but I also know a lot of people much smarter than me are working hard to find out why this is happening to millions of people, and they're finding more treatments. Maybe someday, they'll be able to fix me. In the meantime, I hope I can use what I've learned and experienced to help other people going through the same thing.

Explaining Fibromyalgia to Family and Friends

Sarah Reidle

In the following article Sarah Reidle, the mother of two young children, describes how difficult it is to explain her limitations to them and to her husband, her friends, and to strangers. People do not realize how painful fibromyalgia is, she maintains, and they have to be told that even when a person's illness is invisible, it is real. On the other hand, they get tired of hearing about it when they cannot do anything to help. In Reidle's opinion, it is important for her to show interest in other people's lives and be willing to listen to their problems; then on days when the pain is so overwhelming that she feels a need to talk about it, they will respond. But with strangers, she finds it is best not to offer any more information than they ask for.

Fibromyalgia is a very tough subject to discuss because many people do not understand the severity or intensity of fibromyalgia unless it is directly af-

SOURCE: Sarah Reidle, "How to Explain Fibromyalgia to People Who Just Don't Get It," eHow.com, May 9, 2009. Reproduced by permission. www.ehow.com.

fecting them. I would like to give a few examples of how I explain my fibromyalgia to those who just don't seem to get it . . . my kids, my husband, my friends, a stranger who asks about it. All of these people demand a different approach of explaining my illness.

Explaining to Children or a Spouse

The first scenario . . . for me [involves] finding a way to explain fibromyalgia to my children who are very young: almost 2 and almost 4.

The best way I can advise to talk about fibromyalgia with little kids is to explain that "hey, mommy hurts all the time and you need to be gentle with her." I explained to them that it is not their fault that mommy hurts, but mommy needs you to be gentle with her because she has an owie called fibromyalgia and it's not going to go away, so we need to find new ways to play together so mommy doesn't have to be away from you very much.

Of course, young children need reminders and they aren't going to remember that you hurt 24/7. You may need to remind them by saying something like, "remember mommy's fibromyalgia . . . be gentle on mommy. You can sit with me but you have to sit still and you have to be careful how you climb up." I like to encourage sitting still by offering up reading a book or we watch a movie in daddy's chair . . . all three of us . . . cuddled up under a blanket and have calm time.

Explaining fibromyalgia to a spouse has to be handled almost as gently as explaining it to young children. The best way I have found to explain how I am feelng each day is to put it in man terms. When I am in a bad flare, I tell my husband that I feel like I have been beaten with a sledge hammer and when I finally collapsed after it . . . I was kicked while I was down. Or . . . tell him that my body feels like it did when I bounced all over the back of a station wagon as it flipped end over end.

I have also found that with my husband, if you talk too long about fibromyalgia their eyes seem to glaze over and you can tell they are zoning you out. If you feel he needs to know keep it short and to the point . . . if your spouse is anything like mine, they won't like to hear about an illness that is sucking your energy and strength and they can't do anything about it. However . . . while trying to keep it simple, you don't need to downplay your symptoms to get other people to listen you. With your spouse, it is important that they understand that sometimes you just need to talk about it . . . even if they can't "fix" you.

Explaining to Friends and Strangers

Explaining fibromyalgia to your friends is pretty much the same as explaining it to your spouse. I find that when I catch myself talking too much about my fibromyalgia my friends get tired of my wanting to talk about my body and how it feels. I have made it a point to not talk only about my fibrmyalgia when talking to friends . . . even if that is all I am thinking about.

I have found that showing interest in my friends' lives (like a good friend should) when they have something new—exciting news, disappointing news, or sad news— that my friends are more apt to want to listen when I am having a really bad, need-my-friends kind of day . . . if I am willing to listen to them when they just need to talk. It's very easy to let fibromyalgia monopolize a conversation, but we need to learn when and where it is appropriate to talk about it. If you are having a particularly bad day and just need to talk . . . call a friend and say . . . "do you have time to listen to me talk about my fibromyalgia? I really need to talk about it today because it is just over-

> **FAST FACT**
>
> A 2009 survey of more than one thousand people with chronic pain conducted for HealthyWomen.org shows that more than half of women (53 percent) wish family members would take their chronic pain more seriously, and 31 percent wish that their friends would.

whelming today." I have my mom to talk to about my fibro because she has it too . . . so the same goes for her. . . .

Explaining fibromyalgia to some John or Jane Doe off the street is not always necessary. However, if they are making comments about you or to you, telling you that you shouldn't be feeling that way or whatever, do not hesitate to tell them that you do feel that way.

Whenever some joe shmoe off the street tells me I am too young to feel that way or to be so forgetful or to be walking like I need a cane, I feel the need to say something along the lines of "Yeah, well I do feel that way and I do forget a lot, and I am walking this way because I am sick. I have fibromyalgia and while I may not look sick because I have my hair fixed or I have makeup on, I am sick and if I didn't do my hair and makeup whenever I felt icky, I would never have my hair and makeup fixed. Just because you can't see my illness does not mean that it isn't real because it is." At that point, I let it go unless they want to know more about my illness . . . then I offer up the information they asked for. But only when they ask for it.

Learning to Accept Fibromyalgia

Elizabeth Dudak

In the following viewpoint Elizabeth Dudak tells how hard it was for her to adjust to having fibromyalgia. She had been healthy, athletic, and active with her family, and then suddenly one day she started to have pain. Soon after, her fatigue became so great that she could hardly get out of bed. She became depressed and angry because she could no longer be Supermom to her children. Though her religion had always been important to her, Dudak says, it did not seem to help, and she felt betrayed by God. But she had the support of her family, and when the doctor told her she must take a two-week medical leave from her job, she began to rethink her role in life. She finally realized that she did not need to be Supermom and found that her children enjoyed having her at home with them. Her life has changed dramatically, and she has learned to focus on the good side of the changes rather than the negative ones. Dudak is a writer living in Warrenville, Illinois.

SOURCE: Elizabeth Dudak, "My Battle with Fibromyalgia," *Catholic Digest*, vol. 71, May 2007, pp. 106–07, 109–12. Reproduced by permission.

"**M**om, take it easy. I'll get it for you."

These words spoken by my 13-year-old daughter, Leah, slipped down my spine like ice. I was dreading this moment since being diagnosed with fibromyalgia. I prayed every night that it would never happen. I pleaded with God, Jesus, the saints, and Our Blessed Mother to allow me to remain the person I was before—a healthy, active woman and self-proclaimed Supermom. But when Leah's words hung in the air, I knew I had no choice. At that moment, fibromyalgia had racked my body with pain, fatigue, and guilt; I finally had to succumb to my daughter's assistance.

Fibromyalgia can cause extreme pain throughout the body's muscles, tendons, and ligaments as well as "tender points" that are painful when touched. Another common symptom is acute fatigue. This condition affects women more than men and can last years. To me, having fibromyalgia is like having a horrible flu that includes constant muscle pain and absolutely no energy. That was my diagnosis, and it has changed my life dramatically.

It started on my family's vacation to Mackinaw Island[Michigan]. On one of our bicycle rides back to our rented condo, my knees started to ache. It was odd, but I laughed it off as getting old. I told my husband that my 28 years of playing volleyball had finally taken a toll on me. As the days progressed, the ache became unbearable. It was not the normal knee pain I knew as an athlete; it was a type of pain I'd never experienced before, and it seemed to reach deep into the bone. I bucked it up, as all ex-athletes do, and made the best of the trip.

When we returned, the pain in my knees continued. Fatigue also began, engulfing my entire being. Getting up in the morning was like trying to reach the top of a mountain. Every push to get myself out of bed took mental stamina, and I dragged my body through the rest of each day. My thighs felt heavy, and the pain took over other parts of me, including my elbows, spine, and hips. The pain in my knees worsened—one stab after another after another.

Searching for Answers

I started my visits to various doctors. My general practitioner tested me for a thyroid condition and Lyme disease. I went to a rheumatologist to be tested for rheumatoid arthritis. A neurologist tested me for multiple sclerosis. These were life-altering diseases! Each test result came back negative. While I should have been rejoicing, I instead became depressed and disappointed—I just wanted something tangible so that I could take a pill or something that would make it all disappear. I was consumed with pain and self-pity. To this day, I am not proud of my reactions; I know of women who spend weeks in bed from these life-threatening diseases. I was blessed with these results, yet all I carried was anger and self-pity. I was so wrapped up in trying to continue my role as Supermom that I did not even take note of my selfish disappointment.

Throughout all of this, I continued to pray. Every night I said prayers to God, to Jesus, to St. Jude, to my guardian angel, and to my patron saint, St. Elizabeth of Hungary. I would talk to [St.] Mary on my drive to work, asking her to bargain with God for me. Certainly she would understand that I could not be the mother God wanted me to be unless I fully had my health. If anyone understood the Supermom's role, it was Mary, the greatest mother of all time.

The answers that I wanted did not come, and my frustration grew. Much like a child who gets angry at a parent when she does not get her way, I yelled and cried and screamed. At certain points, I did not attend church. I showed God. If God was not going to grant me my wish—

and that is how I was now seeing Him, a genie—then, why should I worship in his house? I felt betrayed, alone and desperate.

During this time, I was masking my true feelings. I kept telling important people in my life that God put me on the journey for a reason. I convinced them that my faith was strong. I almost convinced myself, too, but the truth would be revealed in the loneliness of the night. It was then when the anger would pour out of me. My prayers were no longer those of faith, but of betrayal and admonishment.

Family Support

I did have the support of family and friends. My mom told me that she prayed for me at her Rosary Society meetings. My sister, Andrea, was there to listen to my tantrums and to assure me God was listening. My children, Leah and

Many religious fibromyalgia sufferers have their faith challenged by the disease. (© Andrew McConnell/Alamy)

Matthew, told me it was OK that I missed a band concert here, an ice-cream social there. I had so many friends and family members who were there for me. My husband, Peter, was my rock. He not only took me to my appointments and listened to my fears; he also played the role of Mr. Mom when I could not. Most importantly, Peter was the one who started to turn this all around for me without even knowing.

After 10 months of pain and fatigue, and exhausting all the doctors and opinions I possibly could, I was lying in bed asking, "Why? Why me? Why now?" I was spouting those questions out loud into the darkness of my room, convinced that I was talking to empty air. As the anger built, I remembered something that Peter had told me I relay to my kids when things aren't going their way: "*No* is an answer," Peter had said, "and you have to have as much acceptance with that answer as you do with *yes*." I do not know why that lesson hit me then and not before. Maybe I was finally starting to listen. That night I began to feel a bit of comfort and less anger.

About a week later, my doctor decided I needed a two-week medical leave. I needed to take a break from the constant physical and mental push it took to get through my day. Throughout all of this, I had still been working 30 hours a week and donning the Supermom's cape as much as possible. I left the doctor's office with a determination to spend my leave truly looking at my life and my priorities, and figuring out where God was calling me. I needed to listen to his answer instead of blocking it out and waiting for mine. I started to really think about my husband's words. Though I do not think God was saying "no" to me, He was answering me in different ways.

During this time, I kept thinking about my calling as a mom. New definitions of motherhood evolved. I started

---

FAST FACT

The term "fibromyalgia" comes from Latin and Greek words. *Fibra* (Latin) means "fibrous tissue," *myos* (Greek) means "muscle," and *algos* (Greek) means "pain."

to let go of the "super" part of mom. I always thought I was being a good mom if I got my kids to all their swim practices and dance recitals and attended every one of their extracurricular events. Now, as fibromyalgia took over more of my life, I physically had to slow down, and in the process other priorities took over. Slowly I began to realize that I was getting my answers.

A New View of Motherhood

Eureka moments started flooding into my brain like a dam had just broken. Trying to be Supermom was an attempt to be the best, but that meaning, in motherhood, constantly changes. I started to have moments in which I sat with my feet propped up and ice packs on my knees, laughing with my daughter about a crazy story her friend told her. Or making fried dough with powdered sugar on top of the stove for my ever sweet-toothed son because I could not get him to the ice cream social. I was still able to comfort and laugh with my children and to be a mom to them.

As I neared the end of my two-week medical leave, my daughter surprised me. If she and her brother cut back on things like camps, new clothes, and eating out, she asked, would I be able to quit my job? They enjoyed me being home with them just *doing nothing*. Then she revealed the hugest eureka moment for me. Since my illness, she said, I had become a better mom. She told me with the honesty only children can possess that since I'd been ill, I hadn't been as crabby. Schedules, commitments, and participation in activities meant less to her than me just being there in the moment.

Leah and Matthew still have commitments that my husband or I have to get them to. I still have to push myself through the day. I still have to juggle all those balls that are tossed at moms and more than likely, because of my fibromyalgia, I will drop some. However, my life has changed so dramatically. I wasted so much of my time concentrating on the negativism of those changes instead of embracing the good. I am a changed person. Parenting has a different meaning.

I still hold some guilt for relying on my children to be my legs. I still cringe when I ask for simple favors because fibromyalgia has taken its toll on me. I can only pray and put faith in God, Mary, and their guardian angels that it makes my children stronger persons. I still pray for the physical life I once knew and will continue to pray for the return of my old physical self. Mostly, I will pray for God's will to be done, whatever He deems that to be, and I will do so with renewed faith.

GLOSSARY

ACR The American College of Rheumatology, an association of physicians specializing in arthritis and similar conditions, which in 1990 developed the classification criteria for fibromyalgia commonly used to diagnose it.

allodynia Pain experienced from stimuli such as touch and temperature that are not normally painful.

alternative or complementary medicine Treatments or medications that are not viewed as traditional and have not undergone a rigorous scientific evaluation.

amitriptyline An antidepressant drug that helps some fibromyalgia patients, even if they are not depressed, by improving sleep. It has been prescribed for many years.

analgesic A pain-relieving medication.

arthritis Inflammation of a joint. Fibromyalgia is often treated by doctors who specialize in arthritis because the pain caused by the two conditions is similar; however, with fibromyalgia, joints are not inflamed.

CFIDS Chronic fatigue and immune dysfunction syndrome, also known as **CFS** for chronic fatigue syndrome. A condition of extreme fatigue that interferes with daily living that has lasted six months or more, along with other symptoms such as pain and sleep difficulties. Because many of these symptoms are similar to those of fibromyalgia, the two are often discussed together.

CNS	Central nervous system—the brain and spinal cord.
Cymbalta	The second drug, after Lyrica, to be approved by the FDA for treatment of pain from fibromyalgia.
disease	A disorder in a system or organ that affects the body's condition consistently, has a recognized cause, and is characterized by an identifiable group of signs and symptoms.
FDA	The Food and Drug Administration, an agency within the U.S. Public Health Service, which is a part of the Department of Health and Human Services. This agency must approve all medicinal drugs before they can be prescribed by doctors.
fibro	A shortened form of the term "fibromyalgia" commonly used by people who have the condition.
fibro fog	A term used by many people with fibromyalgia to refer to the mental confusion and forgetfulness sometimes associated with the syndrome.
fibrositis	A term formerly used for fibromyalgia; it may still appear in older books and articles.
FMS	An abbreviation for "fibromyalgia syndrome."
hyperalgesia	Extreme sensitivity to painful stimuli. Pain response in persons with fibromyalgia is more elevated than in other individuals.
hypochondriac	A person who is abnormally concerned about his or her health and frequently experiences imaginary illnesses. People with fibromyalgia are often suspected of being hypochrondriacs before finding a doctor who correctly diagnoses their condition.

IBS   Irritable bowel syndrome, a common chronic intestinal disorder. It is separate from fibromyalgia but often occurs simultaneously with it and may have similar causes.

Lyrica   The first prescription drug approved by the FDA to treat the pain of fibromyalgia.

musculoskeletal   Pertaining to the ligaments, muscles, tendons, joints, and bones with the associated tissues that move the body and maintain its form.

myalgia   Pain for any reason in one or more muscles.

NSAIDs   Non steroidal anti-inflammatory drugs such as ibuprofen and naproxen, many of which do not require prescriptions. These drugs relieve most types of mild to moderate pain, but they rarely help people with fibromyalgia.

paresthesia   An abnormal skin sensation, such as numbness, burning, or tingling, without an obvious cause. This sensation can result from nerve damage but also occurs in many people with fibromyalgia.

psychosomatic   Physical effects on the body caused by psychological or emotional factors. This term is often used erroneously to refer to imaginary symptoms.

rheumatologist   A physician who specializes in treating arthritis, autoimmune diseases, and fibromyalgia.

Savella   The third drug, after Lyrica and Cymbalta, to be approved by the FDA for treatment of fibromyalgia pain.

syndrome   A collection of signs, symptoms, and medical problems that tend to occur together but are not related to a specific, identifiable cause.

tender points   Specific areas of the body that are very painful in most fibromyalgia patients when gently probed.

trigger points   Tight bands of muscle tissue that are painful to the touch and can cause radiation of pain throughout the body when pressure is applied.

WHO   World Health Organization, the directing and coordinating authority for health within the United Nations system.

CHRONOLOGY

1816   William Balfour, a surgeon at the University of Edin-
        burgh, gives the first full description of fibromyalgia, a
        condition that had been mentioned in nonmedical liter-
        ature since ancient times.

1824   Balfour describes the body's tender points common in
        fibromyalgia.

1880   An American psychiatrist uses the term *neurasthenia* for
        a collection of symptoms consisting of fatigue, wide-
        spread pain, and psychological disturbances, which he
        attributes to the stress of modern life. This becomes the
        prevalent term for such symptoms in the late nineteenth
        and early twentieth centuries, until about the time of
        World War I (1914–1918).

1892   The prominent physician Sir William Osler, in his book
        *The Principles and Practice of Medicine: Diseases of the
        Nervous System*, describes neurasthenia as a condition
        associated with sleeplessness, unhealthy reaction to
        stimuli, weariness on the least exertion, and aching pain.

1904   The term *fibrositis* is coined by Sir William Gowers to
        describe the tender points found in patients with mus-
        cular rheumatism, points that he mistakenly believes
        must be inflamed. It is later used for the entire syn-
        drome now known as fibromyalgia.

1972   Canadian rheumatologist Hugh Smythe publishes a
        description of fibrositis in a widely used textbook,

suggesting that the presence of tender points can distinguish it from conditions that are wholly psychological. This description arouses the interest of researchers and initiates the modern medical view of the disorder.

1975   Smythe and psychiatrist Harvey Moldofsky perform the first sleep electroencephalogram study identifying the sleep disturbances that accompany fibromyalgia.

1976   The term *fibromyalgia* is coined to replace *fibrositis*, which was inaccurate because *itis* means "inflammation." *Fibra* (Latin) means "fibrous tissue," *myos* (Greek) means "muscle," and *algos* (Greek) means "pain."

1981   The first controlled clinical study of fibromyalgia with validation of known symptoms and tender points is published by Muhammad Yunus.

1987   The American Medical Association recognizes fibromyalgia as a real physical condition.

1990   The American College of Rheumatology develops classification criteria for fibromyalgia to be used for research purposes. These soon begin to be viewed as official diagnostic criteria, although not all doctors restrict the diagnosis to patients who meet those criteria.

1993   The World Health Organization (WHO) officially recognizes fibromyalgia as a diagnosis.

1990s   New brain imaging techniques enable researchers to identify sensitization of the central nervous system in fibromyalgia patients.

1997   The National Fibromyalgia Association is established. It is the first national organization with the aim of supporting patients and educating the public about the condition.

2005   The American Pain Society publishes the first guidelines for the management of fibromyalgia pain.

2007   The FDA approves Lyrica for treatment of fibromyalgia pain, the first drug ever specifically authorized for it, drawing widespread media attention. Many patient advocates applaud this event as a major step forward, while critics suggest that the increasing acceptance of fibromyalgia as a medical condition has been influenced by the pharmaceutical industry's expectation of profit.

2008   The antidepressant Cymbalta, which is effective in several pain disorders as well as depression, is approved by the FDA for treatment of fibromyalgia.

2009   Savella, another antidepressant drug also effective for pain relief, is approved by the FDA for fibromyalgia treatment.

2010   A year after the approval of Savella, a consumer advocacy group urges the FDA to recall it on grounds that it was never proven effective for fibromyalgia, was rejected by European regulators, and can cause dangerously high blood pressure.

ORGANIZATIONS TO CONTACT

The editors have compiled the following list of organizations concerned with the issues debated in this book. The descriptions are derived from materials provided by the organizations. All have publications or information available for interested readers. The list was compiled on the date of publication of the present volume; the information provided here may change. Be aware that many organizations take several weeks or longer to respond to inquiries, so allow as much time as possible for the receipt of requested materials.

American Fibromyalgia Syndrome Association (AFSA)
PO Box 32698
Tucson, AZ 85751
(520) 733-1570
fax: (520) 290-5550
www.afsafund.org

The AFSA's primary mission is to fund superior quality scientific studies on fibromyalgia syndrome (FMS). Its Web site contains information about FMS, a fact sheet on fibromyalgia research, and descriptions of projects it has funded.

Fibrocenter
235 E. Forty-second St.
New York, NY 10017
www.fibrocenter.com

Fibrocenter is maintained by the pharmaceutical company Pfizer. It has information about fibromyalgia, getting a diagnosis, and prescription drug treatment, plus personal stories of people with fibromyalgia. Advice about where on the site to find information for school projects is provided, but inquiries are accepted only from persons over eighteen.

Fibrohugs
(480) 264-1058
www.fibrohugs.org

Fibrohugs is a large interactive site run by people who have fibromyalgia, focused on support for others who suffer from it. It features monitored chats and forums, member submissions, many articles, and an extensive list of links.

Fibromyalgia Coalition International (FCI)
6220 Antioch Rd.
Ste. 212
Merriam, KS 66202-5107
(913) 384-4673
fax: (913) 384-8998
www.fibrocoalition.org

FCI is a nonprofit organization focused on support groups, awareness outreach, annual conferences, continuing education for health care professionals, and research efforts. It publishes *Fibromyalgia Alternative News* (*FAN*) magazine and *Conquering the Challenge* newsletter; back issues of both are for sale at its Web site.

Fibromyalgia Information Foundation (FIF)
PO Box 19016
Portland, OR 97280
www.myalgia.com

The FIF is a nonprofit foundation directed by researchers at the Oregon Health & Science University who are engaged in the day-to-day management of fibromyalgia patients or fibromyalgia research. Its aim is to increase the public's understanding of fibromyalgia by providing information based on scientifically validated research studies. Its Web site contains detailed information on what is known about fibromyalgia and on research that is being conducted.

Fibromyalgia Network
PO Box 31750
Tucson, AZ 85751
(800) 853-2929
fax: (520) 290-5550
www.fmnetnews.com

The Fibromyalgia Network's aim is to educate and assist patients with ad-free, patient-focused information that they can put to use. It produces the *Fibromyalgia Network Journal*, monthly eNews alerts, and other support and educational materials available to members. Its Web site includes sample articles plus objective, research-based evaluations of products and treatments that are promoted on the Internet.

Fibrotalk
www.fibrotalk.com

Fibrotalk is a support community run by fibromyalgia patients that offers a forum and chat room. It publishes *Fog Magazine* (www.fogmagazine.com), which is created by a worldwide network of volunteers dedicated to producing quality educational and entertaining material, free of charge, to promote the causes, issues, and support of chronic pain sufferers the world over.

FMS Community
801 Riverside Dr.
Lumberton, NC 28358
www.fmscommunity.org

The FMS Community is part of the Chronic Syndrome Support Association (CSSA), a nonprofit organization founded to educate the general population and health care professionals who lack current knowledge of the research being done on serious, yet invisible, chronic immunological and neurological disorders.

Its Web site includes back issues of its newsletter and many informative articles.

Know Fibro
www.knowfibro.com

This Web site is cosponsored by the National Fibromyalgia Association and the Lilly pharmaceutical company. It contains a self-management guide for people with the condition, the downloadable book *Get to Know Fibro*, and videos about the personal experience of Martha Beck, a fibromyalgia patient.

Men with Fibromyalgia
www.menwithfibro.com

This Web site is devoted to providing information and support to men with fibromyalgia, who often feel neglected at other sites because the condition affects far more women than men. It is focused on an active forum, although articles are also available.

National Fibromyalgia Association (NFA)
2121 S. Towne Centre Pl., Ste. 300
Anaheim, CA 92806
(714) 921-0150
fax: (714) 921-6920
www.fmaware.org

The NFA is a large nonprofit organization whose mission is to develop and execute programs dedicated to improving the quality of life for people with fibromyalgia. It publishes *Fibromyalgia Aware* magazine, of which a free preview of the current issue is offered, and FM Online, available only to members. The site contains extensive information about all aspects of fibromyalgia, including many articles accessible to nonmembers.

National Fibromyalgia Partnership (NFP)
PO Box 160
Linden, VA 22642
(866) 725-4404
www.fmpartnership.org

The NFP is a nonprofit educational organization. It publishes *Fibromyalgia Frontiers*, a quarterly journal for members, and maintains an online supplement at www.frontiersnews.org. Its Web site offers articles about fibromyalgia and many links to resources for patients.

National Fibromyalgia Research Association (NFRA)
PO Box 500
Salem, OR 97302
www.nfra.net

The NFRA is a nonprofit activist organization dedicated to education, treatment, and finding a cure for fibromyalgia. It has raised over $1.6 million toward funding of research, raising of medical and public awareness, and lobbying. Its Web site contains medical information about FMS and news of new developments in research and treatment.

FOR FURTHER READING

Books

Lynette Bassman, *The Feel-Good Guide to Fibromyalgia & Chronic Fatigue Syndrome: A Comprehensive Resource for Recovery*. Oakland, CA: New Harbinger, 2007.

Alison Bested and Alan Logan, *Hope and Help for Chronic Fatigue Syndrome and Fibromyalgia*. Nashville, TN: Cumberland House, 2008.

Dede Bonner and Patrick B. Wood, *The 10 Best Questions for Living with Fibromyalgia: The Script You Need to Take Control of Your Health*. New York: Fireside, 2009.

Tami Brady, *Strategies: A Chronic Fatigue Syndrome and Fibromyalgia Journey*. Ann Arbor, MI: Loving Healing, 2008.

Celeste Cooper and Jeffrey Miller, *Integrative Therapies for Fibromyalgia, Chronic Fatigue Syndrome, and Myofascial Pain: The Mind-Body Connection*. Rochester, VT: Healing Arts, 2010.

David Dryland and Lode List, *The Fibromyalgia Solution: A Breakthrough Approach to Heal Your Body and Take Back Your Life*. New York: Wellness Central, 2007.

Dorothy Foltz-Gray, *The Arthritis Foundation's Guide to Good Living with Fibromyalgia*. Atlanta: Arthritis Foundation, 2006.

M. Clement Hall, *The Fibromyalgia Controversy*. Amherst, NY: Prometheus, 2009.

Kim D. Jones and Janice H. Hoffman, *Fibromyalgia.* Santa Barbara, CA: Greenwood, 2009.

Lynne Matallana and Laurence A. Bradley, *The Complete Idiot's Guide to Fibromyalgia.* New York: Alpha, 2009.

Rodger H. Murphree, *Treating and Beating Fibromyalgia and Chronic Fatigue Syndrome.* Birmingham, AL: Harrison & Hampton, 2009.

Sharon Ostalecki, *Fibromyalgia: The Complete Guide from Medical Experts and Patients.* Sudbury, MA: Jones and Bartlett, 2008.

Sharon Ostalecki and Martin S. Tamler, *100 Questions & Answers About Fibromyalgia.* Sudbury, MA: Jones and Bartlett, 2009.

Jordan Rubin and Joseph Brasco, *Great Physician's Rx for Chronic Fatigue and Fibromyalgia.* Nashville, TN: Thomas Nelson, 2007.

J.G. Schnellmann, *Understanding and Conquering Fibromyalgia.* Charleston, SC: CreateSpace, 2009.

R. Paul St. Amand and Claudia Craig Marek, *What Your Doctor May Not Tell You About Pediatric Fibromyalgia.* New York: Wellness Central, 2006.

Roland Staud, *Fibromyalgia for Dummies.* Hoboken, NJ: Wiley, 2007.

Jacob Teitelbaum, *From Fatigued to Fantastic.* New York: Avery, 2007.

David H. Trock and Frances Chamberlain, *Healing Fibromyalgia.* Hoboken, NJ: Wiley, 2007.

Daniel J. Wallace and Daniel J. Clauw, eds., *Fibromyalgia & Other Central Pain Syndromes.* Philadelphia: Lippincott Williams & Wilkins, 2005.

William Wilke, *The Cleveland Clinic Guide to Fibromyalgia.* New York: Kaplan, 2009.

Periodicals

Bryan Arling, "Health Advice: Will Neurontin Work as Well as Lyrica for Fibromyalgia?" *U.S. News & World Report*, August 19, 2009.

Alex Berenson, "Drug Approved. Is Disease Real?" *New York Times*, January 14, 2008.

Kathleen Doheny, "Take Back Your Energy: Here Are 31 Ways to Control the Pain and Exhaustion of Fibromyalgia," *Natural Health*, October 2005.

Environmental Nutrition, "Ways to Help You Cope with the Aches and Pain of Fibromyalgia," January 2006.

————, "Little Evidence of a Diet Link to Fibromyalgia," February 2009.

Food & Fitness Advisor, "Fibromyalgia Demystified: New Research Shows Those Aches and Pains Are Not All in Your Head—Exercise and Medications Can Help," May 2007.

Jodi Helmer, "Diagnosis: Distress; More and More Lesbians Are Learning to Live with Fibromyalgia," *Curve*, May 2007.

Katherine Hobson, "Gain Against the Pain," *U.S. News & World Report*, October 29, 2007.

Catherine Hollingsworth, "Fibromyalgia Competition Heats Up with FDA Approval of Savella," *Bioworld Today*, January 16, 2009.

Lyle Hurd, "Jacob Teitelbaum, M.D.: Effective Treatment for Chronic Fatigue, Fibromyalgia, Muscle Pain," *Total Health*, May/June 2007.

Kaleb Montgomery, "Blame, Responsibility and Chronic Fatigue/Fibromyalgia," *Acupuncture Today*, September 2009.

New York Times, Letters, "Disease or Not, the Pain Is Very Real," January 17, 2008.

Mehment Oz, "Dr. Oz Will See You Now," *O, The Oprah Magazine*, September 2009.

January W. Payne, "A New Fibromyalgia Remedy: Antiviral Drugs," *U.S. News & World Report*, April 11, 2008.

Melissa Schorr, "Is It All in My Head?" *Psychology Today*, May/June 2005.

N. Seppa, "Origins of Ache: Immune Proteins May Yield Chronic-Pain Clues," *Science News*, August 19, 2006.

Clayton Simmons, "Wake and Ache: Pills for a Puzzling Illness," *Psychology Today*, May/June 2009.

Spirituality & Health Magazine, "Writing Oneself Out of Fibromyalgia," May/June 2009.

Jacob Teitelbaum, "Easing Pain Through Treating Sleep: The Role of Sleep in Effective Treatment of CFS, FMS, and MPS Using a Comprehensive Medicine Approach," *Sleep Review*, April 2009.

Anne Underwood, "Getting to the Roots of Fibromyalgia Pain," *New York Times*, September 23, 2009.

————, "The Long Search for Fibromyalgia Support," *New York Times*, September 23, 2009.

————, "What to Ask About Fibromyalgia," *New York Times*, September 23, 2009.

Women's Health Weekly, "Fibromyalgia Can No Longer Be Called the 'Invisible' Syndrome," November 20, 2008.

————, "Scientists at University of Leon Describe Research in Fibromyalgia," March 5, 2009.

INDEX

PERSPECTIVES ON DISEASES AND DISORDERS